LIGHTING
the WICK

LIGHTING
the WICK

AN INTUITIVE GUIDE TO THE
ANCIENT ART & MODERN
MAGIC OF CANDLES

SANDRA MARIAH WRIGHT
& LEANNE MARRAMA

A TARCHERPERIGEE BOOK

tarcherperigee

an imprint of Penguin Random House LLC
penguinrandomhouse.com

Copyright © 2021 by Sandra Mariah Wright and Leanne Marrama
Illustrations by Lisa Ainsworth

Penguin supports copyright. Copyright fuels creativity, encourages diverse voices, promotes free speech, and creates a vibrant culture. Thank you for buying an authorized edition of this book and for complying with copyright laws by not reproducing, scanning, or distributing any part of it in any form without permission. You are supporting writers and allowing Penguin to continue to publish books for every reader.

Most TarcherPerigee books are available at special quantity discounts for bulk purchase for sales promotions, premiums, fund-raising, and educational needs. Special books or book excerpts also can be created to fit specific needs. For details, write: SpecialMarkets@penguinrandomhouse.com.

Library of Congress Cataloging-in-Publication Data

Names: Wright, Sandra Mariah, author. | Marrama, Leanne, author.
Title: Lighting the wick: an intuitive guide to the ancient art and modern magic of candles /
by Sandra Mariah Wright and Leanne Marrama.
Description: New York: TarcherPerigee, an imprint of Penguin Random House LLC, 2021. |
Includes bibliographical references.
Identifiers: LCCN 2021017336 (print) | LCCN 2021017337 (ebook) |
ISBN 9780593418345 (paperback) | ISBN 9780593418352 (ebook)
Subjects: LCSH: Candles and lights—Miscellanea. | Magic.
Classification: LCC BF1623.C26 W75 2021 (print) |
LCC BF1623.C26 (ebook) | DDC 133.4/3—dc23
LC record available at https://lccn.loc.gov/2021017336
LC ebook record available at https://lccn.loc.gov/2021017337

Printed in the United States of America
1st Printing

Book design by Laura K. Corless

For my husband, Kevin,
Brigid's fire incarnate. Ours is an eternal flame.
For my mother, Joanne, "the fire is Jo,"
a Sagittarius who will remain the guiding light of my life always.
For my teachers, who held the lantern of enlightenment
to illuminate the path of wisdom.
For Wendy, who was brave enough to seek the truth.
For all those I have lit a candle for, and
for all those who have ever lit one for me.
With love and deepest gratitude,
Sandra

✳

For my children, Elizabeth and Kevin, who are the two lights that shone
through darkness and gave me hope. I love you both.
To my parents, Rita and Eddie,
who always encouraged me to shine bright.
I am lucky to be your daughter.
For Chris, who came into my life reigniting love in my soul.
Thank you for helping me find my spark.
"The lights in the sky have finally arrived, I am staying right beside you."
Love,
Leanne

✳

Finally, this is for all the TeaTimers who joined us every morning
when the pandemic hit and the lockdown kept us all quarantined.
We're all here, and we're all safe. ♥

CONTENTS

CONTENTS

INTRODUCTION

"Is there something I can do to protect myself and loved ones?"

"I've been so stressed lately, and my relationship is falling apart. How do I fix it?"

"My friend is sick, and I'm afraid she has the virus. What can I do to help her?"

"What's happening in the world makes me feel so powerless. Is there any kind of spell I can do?"

We are professional psychics based in Salem, Massachusetts, and these and many more questions occupy the minds of our clients. Operating three popular occult shops during a pandemic and widespread civil unrest, we connected every day with people who desperately wanted to help, to do *something.* The concerns our clients share—and the items visitors to our stores continue to purchase—have given us a window into the ways they are hoping to heal, to protect, to secure steady income, and to find peace and happiness again. This book is our chance to reach even more people and give them resources they can work with.

So who are we?

SANDRA MARIAH WRIGHT

I found my way to Witchcraft at a young age; growing up in the Witch city of Salem made it easier. I was raised Catholic, and my favorite religious experience was midnight mass on Christmas Eve. Holding the white taper candle in the hush of the dark church, sing-ing my heart out as the frankincense swirled around me—it's no wonder I became a Witch!

I began practicing Witchcraft when I was still in junior high school. Laurie Cabot had a shop on Essex Street in Salem, and I re-member purchasing the components for my first spell there. Of course, it had to do with a boy. From that first time placing dried herbs and stones into a brightly colored pouch and lighting a candle inscribed with a heart, I began to believe that not only could I look into the future, I could *change* it. Unbeknownst to me, I would come to counsel hundreds of people about their relationships in the years ahead.

In March 2020, I found myself anointing and lighting candles every single morning and evening: one for loved ones who had fallen ill with COVID-19, and one to protect people from the virus. One to help people with the financial distress that came along with the virus, and one to help those who were searching for a vaccine. One for those on the front lines: to guard them, support them, and give them the strength to continue to fight the biggest battle of their lives. The folks who knew I was lighting candles for them felt better, and it made me feel better, too. It made me feel a little less powerless against the invisible enemy that was ravaging life as we knew it.

During the shutdown, Leanne and I began hosting a Zoom meeting to start the day, open to anyone who wanted to learn more about the Craft of the Wise. Guided meditations, Tarot and oracle card pulls, and information about crystals and herbs filled our mornings. We each dove deeper into our personal practice and our love of Witchcraft, and we were happy to share it with others of like mind. At a time when we were all isolated out of necessity, we were doing what we have always done best: bringing people together and bringing the magic.

That May, we released our first book, *Reading the Leaves: An Intuitive Guide to the Ancient Art and Modern Magic of Tea Leaf Divination*. Launching it during such a stressful and strange time was bittersweet, and we wondered how it would be received. Our hearts were touched by the response: people were looking for—and finding—guidance and answers in the bottom of their cups. They were discovering, as we have time and time again, the comfort that can be found in a simple cup of tea. And they were asking us what we were going to write next.

Throughout my life, the Craft of the Wise has provided the support I have needed to overcome obstacles, and I've had the honor of providing many others with the guidance they needed to live their best lives. It is my most sincere wish that this book teaches you a time-honored and effective way to face even the darkest times, with the light of hope and the power of magic.

LEANNE MARRAMA

Candles have illuminated my spiritual and magical life ever since I was a child. Wax adorns the floors of my home as if to say, "Magic lives here." For many of us, candles mark every major occasion. Birthday candles burn brightly, celebrating a new year of life. Christmas and Yule candles promise the birth of the sun/Son. Halloween candles glow within the heart of a pumpkin, reminding us of ancestors who have passed over. On Valentine's Day, dinner is served with pink candles illuminating the romantic scene, radiating love over a shared meal.

Candles are the one tool all religions use. They are my favorite way to work magic, create atmosphere, and pray. The smell of a burning wick brings me back to my childhood and the peaceful feeling of kneeling in church next to my mother. It reminds me that I am not alone, and seeing the smoke rise always lets me know that the heavens are receiving my hopes and prayers.

Like Sandra, I have also used candles to send prayers to help people I love. During the darkest days of COVID-19, my 25-year-old daughter had a grand mal seizure. Watching my child lose control of her body was one of the most terrifying experiences I've had as a mother. Even worse was the fact that I could not travel with her to the hospital for testing and treatment. After dozens of frantic phone calls to friends, a chain of candles and prayers grew, lighting up energy and hope for my family. A warm hug of spiritual light surrounded us, and that love and strength got us through.

When I was first experimenting with Witchcraft at age 18, candle spells were the simplest form of magic I explored. The fire helped me focus my intent and release my energy into the world. Now, so many years later, they are still my go-to tool for harnessing the potential within me, and I have counseled hundreds of clients to do the same. Candle magic empowered me. Read on to find out how it can do the same for you.

CHAPTER 1

THE GIFT OF LIGHT:
A Brief History of Candles

How did this convenient source of light come to have so much spiritual meaning? We're not going to burden you with a long history lesson; we do, however, want to tell the story "from the beginning," because it's fascinating and explains a lot about why candles are such an integral part of so many spiritual practices—and ours in particular.

candle (n.) "cylindrical body of tallow, wax, etc., formed on a wick and used as a source of artificial light," Old English candel "lamp, lantern, candle," an early ecclesiastical borrowing from Latin candela *"a light, torch, candle made of tallow or wax,"* from candere *"to shine,"* from PIE *root* *kand- *"to shine."*

—ONLINE ETYMOLOGY DICTIONARY

SHINING A LIGHT
ON THE ORIGIN OF THE CANDLE

This portable incarnation of the sacred element of Fire has been around in some form for more than 5,000 years, and there is some debate about who gets the credit. Ancient Egyptians had their version, which consisted of reed cores soaked in liquefied animal fat. The Romans rolled sheets of papyrus and dipped them into beeswax or tallow. There are records of candles made from whale fat in China during the Qin dynasty (221–206 BCE). Many equally successful methods were developed independently in India, Japan, and other early civilizations.

Although some cultures soon developed oil lamps that eliminated the need for candles, they remained a popular choice that eventually spawned entire industries. In thirteenth-century England and France, candlemakers (called "chandlers") would travel to homes to create candles from residual kitchen fats, and homemade candle shops popped up, too. Candles served a practical purpose then, and they still do today. So when did they become more than mundane, everyday light sources?

THE GIFT OF THE GODS

Candles carried the power of Fire safely into the home, bringing vital light and heat but also something more: a symbol of the power of the Gods, whomever They were believed to be. To understand the magical significance of candles, we have to acknowledge the unequaled influence of what Aristotle defined as one of the four essential elements of life: Fire. (The others being Earth, Air, and Water.)

You may have learned the myth of Prometheus in school, like we did, but in case you didn't, the ancient Greeks explained how humans acquired fire this way: Zeus told Prometheus to give all newly created creatures of the earth abilities that would help them survive the struggle of life on the planet. The animals and insects were given advantages such as fur, fangs, fins, and wings. By the time man reached the front of the line, all the cool stuff was gone. Prometheus, known to be tricky and maybe too clever for His own good, had an idea. He stole fire, which had not been part of the deal, and snuck it to man in a hollow fennel stalk (reminiscent of a candle!). Zeus was so furious, He punished Prometheus eternally for his wrongdoing. Some stories also say this is how women came to exist: Zeus ordered Hephaistos to create the first woman, Pandora, in the wake of this transgression. We all know how that turned out, right? She's blamed for letting loose all the strife in the world, the way Eve was blamed for taking a bite out of the fruit of the tree of knowledge. The story of Prometheus, and by extension, Pandora, served as a harsh warning not to underestimate the value, destructive capabilities, power, or consequences of Fire.

The scientific explanation of the origin of Fire links it with a random act of nature along those same formidable lines: a lightning strike. Anthropologists estimate the first use of fire was 1,420,000 years ago, but it wasn't until the Neolithic period that humans learned to generate it themselves by using friction, or striking flint on pyrite. Fire directly improved early humans' chances of survival. They used it to stay warm, cook food, direct quarry when hunting, and control enemies when waging war. Eventually, they found it could be used to kill insect pests and clear nuisance vegetation to make stalking prey easier. The benefits were numerous: the burned areas came back first as grasslands that attracted more game and later led to key practices in agriculture, including fire being used to clear land for planting, with the ash as a good fertilizer. Fire was the gift that kept giving, and it still does.

A PERPETUAL, HOLY FLAME

The Statue of Liberty, formally named "Liberty Enlightening the World," holds her torch aloft at the entrance of the United States, a beacon of hope since 1886. Emma Lazarus's famous poem, "The New Colossus," mounted at the entrance to the statue's pedestal describes her as "A mighty woman with a torch, whose flame / Is the imprisoned lightning, and her name / Mother of Exiles. From her beacon-hand / Glows world-wide welcome . . ." Liberty's light is reminiscent of the holy eternal fires of ancient Rome and Greece that gave birth to the Olympic Torch, whose flames were traditionally lit by using a convex mirror to concentrate the sun's rays. That practice is still maintained today, and the torch is still lit in front of the temple of Zeus and Hera.

Likewise, Sandra's ancestral home of Ireland maintains more than one perpetual sacred fire, originally lit in Kildare during the pre-Christian era in honor of Brigid, goddess of the hearth. The fire later became dedicated to St. Brigid, and her nuns tended it, managing to keep it lit despite several attempts to extinguish it, right up until the sixteenth century. It was relit in 1993 and remains burning at Solas Bhride in Kildare, tended by the Brigidine Sisters. A second flame has been lit from that one, which resides in the town square. (Leanne's mother has a souvenir candle from her visit to the eternal flame, where she met the "Witch nuns," her amusing but rather accurate term for the caretakers.) As of this writing, man-made eternal flames are burning in North and South America, Europe, Australia, Asia, Africa, and the Caribbean.

A force of both creation and destruction, Fire has been revered for its capabilities since ancient times, and it has rightly developed into a symbol of holiness, sovereignty, and enlightenment (which literally means "to bring into the light," where light has become synonymous with understanding, wisdom, and clarity). Fire has enjoyed a prominent place in religious practices through the ages that persists to this day.

THE LIGHT OF SPIRITUALITY

Candles are the stars of countless holy days—integral to marking annual events like Hanukkah and Diwali, as well as weekly observances like the Jewish Shabbat. In fact, candles are a part of celebrations in every major religion, so they've likely been with you for many key moments, no matter what your beliefs are, or were in your childhood. As our families practiced Catholicism, we were no strangers to lighting votive offering candles in the vestibule of the church as children. (To this day, Sandra will make a pilgrimage to the 35-foot bronze and copper statue of Madonna Queen of the Universe National Shrine in East Boston to light a votive in the grotto for any Catholics in need of magical assistance, as the lines between magic and prayer are blurry at times.)

In many Christian denominations, candles are often lit as part of prayer requests; the light is equated with Christ. Light, too, has been seen as a sign of holiness for thousands of years—that's where the halos around the heads of saints and other holy figures in centuries of Christian art come from. In Buddhism, candles are a symbol of enlightenment. In Judaism, they are a sign of peace, calm, and reverence. And in Witchcraft, they are a combination of all these things and more: they are seen as a conduit to the powers that can influence our existence; they can represent our deities on the altar and also serve as a way to honor them; they are a way to alter the atmosphere of a space to sanctify it; and they are physical tools that can help purify, bless, and even destroy objects.

One of the most popular goddesses among modern-day Witches is Hecate, who is commonly depicted holding two torches. The history, iconography, and worship of Hecate in Her many forms would fill its own book, but we would be remiss not to address Her here specifically as the light-bringer. Her torches symbolize the divine light of protection: among the many Greek myths of Hecate, one describes how She saved Byzantium from an attack on a moonless night by warning its inhabitants with a mystical light in the sky. They also symbolize wisdom, discernment, and divine guidance. Hers are the liminal spaces between; She is the goddess of the crossroads, lighting the way in this world and the next with Her torches; a psychopomp, guiding souls in their travels to and from the underworld. Truth be told, when we look at our lovely Lady Liberty, standing at the gateway to the United States, we think of Hecate.

DID WOMEN INVENT THE FIRST "SPELL CANDLES"?

In early American history, women—who were in charge of making the 400-plus candles their homes would require in a typical year—pioneered the production of a better-smelling candle. Candles made of animal fat, or tallow, emitted a foul scent when they burned, as you might imagine, and smoked up the place something awful. In keeping with the adage that necessity is the mother of invention, these determined women conjured up a sweet-smelling wax that burned cleaner than tallow by boiling native bayberries. (Can't you just see them standing over their cast-iron cauldrons, stirring up a bubbling brew that would become a blessing in more than one way?)

These candles took a lot of sweat equity to make, and the investment required to create them made them special, linking them to good fortune, prosperity, and abundance, and making them the perfect gift for loved ones. Sandra maintains this centuries-old tradition with her coven and friends, gifting bayberry candles in the holiday season to burn on New Year's Eve to welcome in good luck for the coming year. Passed down through the generations, the idea is to light the candle after dark (some say "when the first star is seen") so it stays lit past midnight to carry its light and blessings into the new year. Don't blow it out—that's bad luck. Keep it where it can safely burn all the way down. The lore is captured in this rhyme: "A bayberry candle burned to the socket brings luck to the home and wealth to the pocket."

Because these candles took quite a bit of time and effort to make, their popularity declined in favor of other methods. With new developments in industry and technology, candle-making ingredients changed, too. Some, like beeswax, are still popular today.

THE MAGIC OF CANDLES

You've been trusting candles with your wishes since the first time you blew them out on your birthday cake. In the coming chapters, we explain what the various types of candles are used for; how to bless and dress candles to be used in meditations, rites, and spellwork; and even how to create your own candles if you are so inclined. We also share some spells from our personal grimoires and give you all the tools you need to create your own. Our mission is to share a bit of our light with you, passing the torch so the eternal flame of magic remains a guiding light to seekers always.

CHAPTER 2

THE SPARK:
What Makes a Candle Magical?

The modest act of lighting a candle with intention is magic. Candles harness the power of Fire—and the fire within a person. Fire is a difficult element to control, both magically and mundanely. Fire can giveth, and fire can taketh away like nobody's business, and it bears to mention that it must be shown great respect. A flame that has been empowered using the techniques in this chapter can transform a situation, or even a person, illuminating difficult and dark situations so we can better manage our life path.

A lit spell candle is the representation of all five sacred elements: the wax is formed by substances of Earth, the flame itself is Fire. Air feeds the flame, which in turn causes Water vapor, seen as the blue base of the flame, and the blessing activates the magic through Spirit.

Lighting a candle represents devotion, truth, wisdom, virtue, grace, personal power, and the providential presence of the Universe. When a person uses candles to enhance their lives, they are extending their own limitless potential to make things happen. Fire combined with your energy, determination, and intention makes even the most ordinary candle magical—and all the elements you choose to add create something special, even formidable. The oils, herbs, spoken words, and related components we discuss heighten the effectiveness of the spell.

CANDLE TYPES

CHIME AND TAPER CANDLES

Chime candles are small, tapered candles that burn quickly, typically within two or three hours. They are available in an array of colors. Sometimes they are used to supplement other, larger candles.

Taper candles are tall, thin candles and come in a large assortment of colors. You can estimate the burn time by the height: figure one hour per inch. Taper candles can easily be inscribed, or anointed and dressed with herbs, and are wonderful for a romantic dinner or love spell. (Why not try both?)

ASSORTED FIGURE CANDLES

Figure candles come in shapes designed to depict people and their relationships or represent iconic images traditionally associated with magic, such as the skull and crossbones, black cat, cross, a stack of seven spheres known as a knob candle, and so on. If you're familiar with figure candles, when you see one burning, you can easily identify the type of work being done—and even if you're unfamiliar with them, you can probably make some educated guesses. If it's a candle where two people are facing each other or embracing, it's most likely a love spell. If they are back to back, it's about parting ways. There are advantages and disadvantages to using such literal portrayals. If you are hoping to keep your goals a secret, you'll need to be sure to work with these in a location where they won't be seen by others.

A **tealight** is a candle in a cup and can dissolve entirely when burned. They are typically small, circular, and often wider than their height.

A NOTE ABOUT SHARING YOUR CANDLE MAGIC ON SOCIAL MEDIA

Countless photos of candle spells exist online, especially on image-based platforms. As tempting as it may be to share your work, it may be better to wait until the spell has manifested the desired outcome before doing so. When you are still hoping to accomplish your goal, it makes sense to protect your endeavor against the envy of others.

Most burn for three or four hours; longer-burning tealights are called nightlights. Tealights aren't typically inscribed or dressed with herbs, but they can be anointed by rubbing the oil on the top, avoiding the wick. We use tealights to send healing, but they can be used for any type of single-candle spellwork.

A **votive candle,** or prayer candle, is a small, thick candle with a flat base often used as a prayer offering. They are either cylindrical or square, often 2 inches tall by 1½ inches in diameter. Votives can easily be inscribed, anointed, or dressed with herbs. Their width allows them to stand without support, so they can be set into a dish rather than a hurricane glass—although if they are set into a glass, they will burn longer. If they stand alone, the wax is prone to run, which allows it to be read for divination purposes.

Pillar candles are cylindrical candles that are both tall and wide. Because they have more wax available to fuel the flame, they can be burned for an extended period of time. There are many ways to use pillar candles, and they come in an assortment of widths and heights. Like votives, they can stand on their own and are often used in wax readings.

TEALIGHT, VOTIVE, PILLAR, 7-DAY, AND JAR CANDLES

Jar candles are wax poured into a glass container and come in as many sizes and shapes as there are different types of jars. Because they're inside a container, they are safer than taper candles for lengthy burning. Most are poured into canning jars or other deep, wide glass containers. Jar candles last a long time and can be relit again and again, which makes them perfect for intense spell and devotional work.

Seven-day candles, which are designed to be burned over a period of—you guessed it—seven days, are popular for novenas, worship, and magical work. The glass container encloses the melted wax, which makes the candle last longer.

SAFE-CANDLE CODE

◆ The most important rule: never leave burning candles unattended, especially in a home where children or animals are present.

◆ Be mindful of what is near the candle. Keep flammable fabrics and fibers away.

◆ Always use a heat-safe holder or dish and handle it with care because it may become hot to the touch.

◆ If you are going to use the candle more than once . . .

» Trim the wick to ½ inch long each time. This cuts down on the soot in the air.

» Plan to burn pillar candles for one hour per inch in diameter to allow the entire surface to melt, which keeps the center of the candle from shrinking down inside the walls (sometimes called "tunneling").

◆ Use a snuffer to extinguish candles rather than blowing them out. Different occult philosophies exist regarding this practice, but our reasoning is practical: blowing out a candle can cause the wick to shift or wax to splatter. Safety first, always.

WHAT IS CLEANSING AND CHARGING A CANDLE, AND CAN ANYONE DO IT?

You don't have to consider yourself a Witch to cleanse and charge a candle, crystal, or any other object. You just have to understand how energy works and why these things are done.

To cleanse a candle is to clear it of any residual energy it may have picked up in its travels. Prior to working with a candle, you can pass it through the smoke of frankincense and myrrh, sage, or palo santo, depending on what's a part of your spiritual practice.

To charge a candle is to imbue it with energy to prepare it for spellwork. This sets it apart from a candle you might use, for example, when the electricity goes out. Some people place candles in moonlight or lay them on an object (like a selenite charging plate); this is a **passive** way to charge a candle because it absorbs energy from light or from an object that is not deliberately, consciously directing it. It is a general blessing.

To charge the candle for a specific spell, use an **active** method, such as holding the candle between your palms and focusing your intent on it. If you can focus and feel your energy, you can charge a candle. If you have never felt your own energy, here is one way to explore it: clap your hands and rub them together for ten seconds. Hold your palms about 1 inch apart, move them to about 5 inches apart, and back to about 1 inch apart. Note how you can feel your hands getting closer and moving away. If you have a hard time feeling it with your eyes open, close them, which should make it easier. This helps you practice channeling your power through your hands.

To charge the candle both actively and passively, you can lay it on the charging plate and place your dominant hand (the hand you write with) over it, sending the energy through your palm.

You can use these methods to prepare your candles before doing any of the spells in this book.

Here are some additional active methods you can use to layer even more energy into the candle:

* **Inscribe it:** This is the act of carving symbols, numbers, words, or any combination of these into the candle with a sharp implement, such as a large-head pin, a letter opener, or a knife. Whatever you choose to inscribe your candles with, cleanse and bless it, and set it aside to be used for that purpose only. Some teachings state you should carve whatever symbols or words indicate your intent in a specific way, such as in a certain direction or without lifting the tool out of the wax until the inscription is complete. These methods serve a purpose: they make the act of inscribing the candle a conscious effort that differs from your typical writing style, which helps you focus your intent even more deliberately. If you are looking to banish something, write from the bottom of the candle to the top, from the closest point to your body to the farthest away. If you are looking to manifest something, write from the top to the bottom, from the farthest point from you to the closest. If you are drawing a single symbol, you may choose to draw it closer to you or farther away, depending on your intention. Try to

keep the implement in contact with the candle the entire time you're carving to maintain the energy you're directing. The following image shows the symbols associated with the Seven Sacred Planets and the four elements. (See the Table of Correspondences on page 220 for a larger list of symbols.)

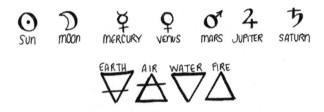

**SYMBOLS OF THE SEVEN SACRED PLANETS
AND THE FOUR ELEMENTS**

* **Anoint it with oil:** This infuses the candle with the essence of the herb or plant the oil is made from. We're not going to get into a debate about fragrance versus essential oils here, but if you're going to use fragrance oils, you may want to infuse them with herbs so they contain the potency of the plant itself, not just the scent: on the third day of a new moon, pour the fragrance oil into a jar, add the herbs, and let them steep. On the full moon, pour the infused oil into another jar through cheesecloth or a fresh coffee filter to strain out the plant matter. (You can dry these herbs and use them in a spell sachet later.) To anoint your candles, place three drops of the oil on your fingertips, usually your pointer and middle fingers, and work it onto the candle. **If you are manifesting something, turn the candle clockwise; if you are banishing**

something, turn it counterclockwise. **If you are drawing something into your life, draw the energy into the middle of the candle** by touching the oil to the top and moving to the middle and then by touching the bottom and moving to the middle, coating the entire candle without drenching the wick. **To send something away, move the energy from the middle of the candle outward.** Start by tapping the oil in the middle of the candle, move to the top, and then move from the middle of the candle to the bottom. As you do this, concentrate on the purpose and imagine the energy moving. You can also choose to speak these words: **"I conjure this candle of magical art to [draw into my life/send away] _____."** You can adjust this statement to match whatever purpose you are dedicating the candle to, and it will add another layer of energy to the working.

A TAPER CANDLE ROLLED IN A DISH OF DRIED HERBS

19

* **Dress it with herbs:** Many teachings call for adding actual dried herbs to the candle as a way to include even more power in the spell. Be careful to keep them away from the wick because they can easily catch on fire, which may cause the flame to shoot up higher than you would expect. You can choose a single herb or create an herb blend that will help specifically target your intention. (See the Table of Correspondences on page 220 for our recommendations.) Rather than just sprinkling them onto the candle, try laying the herbs in a special dish and rolling the candle in them.

THE SALEM WITCHES' WAY TO CREATE YOUR OWN CANDLE SPELL

1. Articulate your desire as specifically as you can. Writing it down helps.

2. Determine the best timing for this work: day of the week? Phase of the moon?

3. Decide on the correct size and shape of the candle(s) to suit the duration of the spell.

4. Choose the color of the candle based on your intention.

5. Cleanse and charge the candle.

6. Conduct any additional steps to imbue the candle with your energy: inscribe, anoint, or dress.

7. When the time is right, prepare yourself and your space, and begin.

CANDLE GRIDS

Those of us who work with crystals know the power they bring to our spells. They make especially useful partners when it comes to candle magic, partly because they add another of the planet's natural gifts to our workings, but also because the smaller stones are portable, allowing us to take the energy of our candle magic with us wherever we go.

A candle grid is a lot like a crystal grid, which is an array of stones organized into a recognizable pattern that holds meaning, intended to support and amplify the force of the crystals toward a goal. Common grid templates include a spiral, the seed of life, the flower of life, the hexagram, Metatron's cube, and other meaningful geometric shapes that correspond to various intentions.

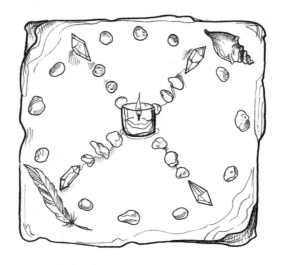

A CANDLE GRID WITH CRYSTALS

If you have ever laid out a crystal grid, this will be easy for you: instead of a focus stone in the center, place your main candle there. You may also place smaller candles along the compass lines, at the quarters, or in other spots depending on your purpose and the size of the grid. If you have never worked with crystal grids, you can explore them with a simple pattern: place your prepared spell candle in the center. Charge 4 crystal points and 12 other tumbled stones that are linked to the spell's purpose. (See the Table of Correspondences on page 220 for our suggestions.) Place a crystal point, facing the candle, at each of the four compass directions. Encircle the candle and connect the cardinal points using the tumbled stones. Sit with the grid and take some deep breaths, feeling the energy of the stones as they channel power to the candle. Then, when you're ready to send the message to the Universe, begin by lighting the wick.

THE CORNERSTONES OF CANDLE MAGIC

Know: Take the time to learn the basics and understand what a spell can and cannot do.

Specify: Be explicit regarding your desires. Make sure your intentions are comprehensive.

Plan: Research what you need to create the appropriate formula to produce results.

Believe: Have confidence in your ability to achieve your goal. Visualize victory.

Live it: Partner real–life action with your spellwork. Align your thoughts, words, and deeds.

Let go: Obsessing over the outcome only smothers the magic. Set it free and carry on.

CHAPTER 3

CANDLES RADIATE WARMTH:
Friendship, Love, Passion, and Cooperation

As the song goes, "Light of the world, shine on me, love is the answer." (Thank you, England Dan and John Ford Coley.) Our relationships have always been important to us, and now more than ever we have been shown just how vital they are. Relationships, or lack thereof, are the number one reason people seek out magic, and candles are the most popular tool we recommend. Candles help a person find, kindle, sweeten, spice up, repair, and even end unhealthy relations.

Love itself is a form of magic. The act of loving another person—whether a lover, family member, or friend—is the most powerful gift we can give. Love magic can work wonders. We have seen it transform connections, heal the wounds of the past, open the door to new loving relationships, or even light the way for a lover's return. Using candle magic empowers you to let your own love light shine. But magic is not to be undertaken lightly. Before beginning any work, you'll need to have a clear picture of what it can and cannot do, and you'll want to build the most important relationship first: the one you have with yourself.

FACTS: BEFORE YOU DO LOVE MAGIC, UNDERSTAND THIS

Despite what you may have heard, you cannot force a person to love you. One person cannot change another person's true will, and even if you could, would you want to? Would you want to live your life knowing you had to drag someone into a relationship? Would you want someone to force you to love them if you didn't feel anything for them? We are all about consent in our mundane philosophies, and our magical philosophies are no different: if you're *currently* in a relationship with a person and you are hoping to strengthen it, that's fair. But you should be wary of any love spell to link you with a specific person who has never expressed, or has lost, interest.

We have had countless clients come to us for advice regarding a crush they pursued who was, by all evidence, completely indifferent. And we've had those same clients return to us, again and again (after not following our advice), hoping against hope to change that person's mind. No matter how many times we advised that their target had good reasons for not wanting to enter into a relationship (everything from already being in love with someone else to being attracted to a different gender) they would persist in trying to capture that person's heart.

Maybe the object of your affection is already in love with another person or attracted to another gender. If so, you're wasting energy—and wax. It would be better to cast a wider net, writing the fine print not on *whom* you want specifically but on what qualities, characteristics, and common interests you'd like your companion to have . . . and one of them should be that they are ready for a relationship and will be attracted to and interested in *you* for who you are.

Unfortunately, we've also had clients who have sought us out because someone they thought loved them betrayed, harmed, or abused them in some way. A candle isn't going to fix disrespect or cruelty. It would be better to burn them out of your life altogether. When there has been repeated disrespect, dishonesty, or infidelity, it's time to put an end to the toxic relationship. We said before that love is the greatest gift you can give another person; it's also the best one you can give yourself. Walking away from what no longer serves you is taking back your power. Save the pink and green candles so you can learn to treasure yourself, and don't settle for anything less than you deserve.

SHINE YOUR LOVE LIGHT
WHERE IT CAN BE SEEN

Before beginning love magic, think first: What have you done to bring love and friendship into your life? Leanne had a client who would buy candles for love magic weekly but then complain that the spells never worked. Leanne asked, "What are you doing to seek out romance?" They replied, "Burning candles." This person had not entered into any situations where they might meet people or even changed the route they took from home to work and back. They had a friendship circle, but it was the same group of people for more than 10 years.

Spells for new love only work if a person is putting themselves out there. If a person is just sitting at home, spellwork alone is not going to cut it. If you were hoping for a new job, wouldn't you look at some job listings? Brush up your résumé and interview skills? Network with people in your field? Talk to people in the positions you are qualified for to see if they knew of any openings? You wouldn't just light a candle and hope a job fell into your lap while you sat on your couch bingeing Netflix, would you?

What we put out into the world returns to us. There have to be opportunities to meet new people somehow for love to come organically. Be brave. Try new experiences. Once a person widens their social circle and interests, the opportunities to find soul mates and friends become endless. Light candles, absolutely, because it helps you focus on what it is you truly want, puts those desires out into the Universe, and enlists help from the realms of Spirit. But follow through with mundane actions that give the magic something to work with and you'll get results.

What happened with that client of Leanne's? They hit it off with someone they met at a computer class, and they are still together as of this writing.

A BASIL PLANT AND CANDLE FOR A SOUL MATE LOVE SPELL

SOUL MATE LOVE SPELL

Finding love takes patience; true love requires patience, so perhaps that's why.

Anyone wanting immediate results is missing the point of how true love grows. Love takes time. People who start throwing around the word *love* after a week or two, without getting to know the person they are saying it to, are either mistaking infatuation for love or using the words to get what they want. We've got spells for hooking up, but this isn't one of them. This is a spell to be used for what William Butler Yeats called "the old high way of love" in his poem "Adam's Curse." This is for the real deal. It requires more than simply lighting a candle. Much like love, it must be cherished, appreciated, and nurtured in order to flourish.

You need:
Pink taper candle
Heat-safe holder
Letter opener or other implement for carving
Rose oil or Venus oil (see Resources in the Appendix)
2 cups potting soil or dirt
4×4-inch square of paper (parchment preferred)
Pink or green pen (pink and green are the colors attributed
  to the planet and the Goddess Venus)
Seeds for a plant (Leanne uses basil because it is easy to
  grow and is often used in love spells, but any seeds
  would work.)
Planting pot
Pink satin mojo bag
Optional additional stones or herbs (see the list on
  page 32)

On a Friday, begin the spell by writing on a piece of paper all that you seek and need in a relationship. Describe the attributes, characteristics, interests, and behaviors you'd appreciate in a companion. Be as detailed as possible, without referring to any person in particular. Do not be afraid to include sexual attraction. Leanne has done this spell, leaving out the sexual attraction, and found several "soul friends" this way. (Of course, sometimes love is discovered through good friends you meet along the way; magic always finds a path.)

Carve the name of the person seeking love into the candle, and include a heart and the symbol of Venus (see the "Symbols of the Seven Sacred Planets and the four elements" figure in Chapter 2). Anoint the candle with rose oil or Venus oil. While rubbing the candle with oil, speak out loud with confidence the attributes you wrote (for example, honest, compassionate, kind, humorous, attentive, successful, single). Place the taper in the heat-safe holder. While the candle burns, place 1 cup of potting soil in the planting pot. Fold the paper, tuck it into the dirt, and cover the paper with the remaining cup of soil. Push three seeds into the dirt in a triangle shape, and cover them lightly. After they are planted, speak the following words:

"Lovely Venus, Evening Star,
  Guide my soul mate from afar.
  On your day, I plant the seed
  And speak the truth of what I need.
  From my heart, my spirit flows
  Sure as this little seedling grows.
  Love of my life, I conjure thee!
  I beckon you to come to me!"

Put the plant near a window that will allow the sun's rays to feed it. Care for this plant, following the directions specific to its type. Investing the time for the seedling to germinate sends a message to the Universe that you are ready for a love that is worth the wait.

Allow the candle to burn all the way down. This may take more than one session of burning it; if it does, always relight it on a Friday. Place any combination of the stones or herbs from the following list in the pink satin mojo bag with the leftover candle wax. When the herb plant grows, you can trim some of the leaves to place in the pouch as well. Anoint the mojo bag by dabbing oil onto it, and carry it with you every day.

Love Crystals

Rose quartz: *Affection, peace, and harmony*
Rhodochrosite: *Stability, self-worth, and compassion*
Chrysoprase: *Soul connection*

Love Herbs

Basil: *Harmony and growth*
Cardamom: *Affection, lust, and fidelity*
Jasmine or hibiscus: *Sensual love and sexual attraction*
Rose: *Love, friendship, and trust*

A BOUQUET OF
SIMPLE CANDLE MEDITATIONS
FOR SOWING AND GROWING LOVE

Choose a single candle in a heat-safe holder, and plan to sit quietly and focus on your intentions.

PINK

Igniting a pink candle sets the stage for love and friendship. When doing this on a Friday, a person opens themselves to intimacy and kindness. While the pink candle is aflame, say the words, "I welcome nurturing love from the Universe."

GREEN

Illuminating a green candle brings abundance, self-love, and affection to those who seek. While burning this candle on a Friday, say the words, "I welcome the gifts of lavishness, tenderness, and love from the Universe."

RED

Burning a red candle on a Tuesday incites passion, seduction, and action; creates an irresistible energy around you; and fuels the confidence and intensity for sex and lust. As the red candle is burning, say the words, "I celebrate my sexuality. I welcome desire from the Universe."

YELLOW

Striking fire to a yellow candle brings needed communication, maturity, and happiness to a person when they are feeling down. While burning this candle on a Sunday, healing and hope will begin to scorch away depression and self-doubt. When the candle is lit, say the words, "I will speak my truth. I welcome hope for the future and healing from the past."

WHITE

Light a white candle to clear away unwanted energy from the past. This helps when romantic love and friendship have grown stagnant or distressed. While burning this candle on a Monday, forgiveness and healing can take place in troubled relationships. When the candle is lit, say the words, "I release the past and welcome healing and new beginnings in my life."

BLUE

Light a blue candle to bring peace, accomplishment, and clarity to your love life. This guides loving relationships to a healthy place. While burning this candle on a Thursday—when the Universe brings loving guidance to relationships—say the words, "I create my own clarity and peace. My relations will attain harmony and success."

WELCOME HOME CANDLE SPELL

See the curtains hangin' in the window
In the evening on a Friday night
A little light-a-shinin' through the window
Lets me know everything's all right . . .

—"SUMMER BREEZE" BY SEALS & CROFTS,
WRITTEN BY JIM SEALS AND DASH CROFTS

Welcoming someone into your house with the light of a candle sends a message of love. Using a scented jar candle is easy and puts a smile on the face of anyone coming through your door, whether they're returning home or just coming to visit.

More specifically, a red candle by the entryway can rekindle passion, and a pink one can open the door to new love and new friends. Add in a bit of chocolate (prized for its aphrodisiac properties for hundreds of years) and maybe even some fresh flowers (roses are classic, but many others, like peonies or carnations, also are associated with love), and you've got the makings of a truly warm welcome or a beautiful offering to spirit.

You need:
    Scented jar candle (pink or red)
    Piece of wrapped chocolate
    Fresh flowers in a vase nearby

On a Friday during the waxing moon, choose a safe spot on a stable surface near your door. Bonus if there's a window, but safely secure any curtains out of the way. Place the jar candle, chocolate, and flowers (if applicable) within reach. Light the candle while making this simple statement to the Universe, "I welcome love with love." Offer the candy to your lover when they come through the door.

SWIPE RIGHT, HOOK UP TONIGHT ATTRACTION CANDLE SPELL

Attraction does not always become love, nor does it need to. An attraction candle spell brings charm and seduction to the person looking for some fun without the commitment. This should *not* be used to find love. Meant for a person who is already engaged in a friendly flirtation, this type of candle magic only enhances the energies and increases the seductive abilities. This builds on the energy of mutual attraction and heightens the magnetism and captivation that already occurs between two—or more—people. (Whatever floats your boat.) What happens after is all about consent and desire.

Note: this spell is intended to help influence people and seduce them without harm. Before you do this spell, take the time to confirm in your mind exactly what you are hoping to achieve. If any part of you is looking for a long-term relationship, this is not the spell for you.

The flame of the candle heats up sexual attraction, while the color red promotes the passionate fun that will follow. The combination of the fire and oils have quite the effect on the ready, willing, and able. The unusual scent soothes self-doubt and is alleged to help relieve sexual hang-ups. Ylang-ylang is a fragrant aphrodisiac, and the spicy scent of ginger is stimulating and encourages daring exploration. Cinnamon does double duty: it contains dopamine, a chemical that can help relax the mind, and it stimulates blood flow—so it helps people chill out *and* heat up.

You need:

Red candle

Heat-safe holder

Letter opener or other pointed implement for carving

2 drops cinnamon oil

2 drops ginger oil

3 drops ylang-ylang oil

1 tablespoon almond oil or grapeseed oil

Red satin mojo bag

On a Tuesday or a Friday, carve your name in the candle. Engrave the symbols for Mars and Venus in the candle (see the "Symbols of the Seven Sacred Planets and the four elements" figure in Chapter 2), the combination of romance and beauty with sexuality and power. Mix the oils together, and anoint the candle with the combination, then place it in the holder.

Think seductive thoughts, and if you are able to place the candle in the center of the room and safely move around it, do so. Move your body, or sit and run your hands over your body, and chant the following words over and over, at least 10 times:

"I am desire,
Passion and fire!"

Burn the candle to completion. Use the remaining oil blend on your own skin (do a patch test first to test for sensitivity) or drip into a bath. Do not put the oil on genitals or other vulnerable areas because cinnamon and ginger commonly irritate skin. Place any combination of the stones or herbs from the following list into the red satin mojo bag with the leftover candle wax. Anoint the mojo bag, and carry it with you when you are looking to hook up.

Attraction Crystals

Garnet: Passion and strength

Carnelian: Vitality and stamina

Ruby: Confidence and leadership

Attraction Herbs

Clove: Luck, supremacy, and control

Cinnamon: Desire, relaxation, passion, and sex

Damiana: Lust, sex, and fascination

Ginger: Passion and magnetism

Ylang-ylang: Desire, relaxation, and craving

Jasmine: Confidence and attractiveness

SWEET, SWEET PASSION CANDLE SPELL

If the daily grind has gotten you and your mate stuck in a rut, this spell can be used to rekindle the flame.

You need:

Red candle

Heat-safe holder

Small food-safe dish

Red rose petals

Jasmine oil

2 strawberries

2 tablespoons honey

Anoint the red candle with jasmine oil. Dot the excess jasmine oil on your pulse points (do a patch test first to check for sensitivity). Place the candle in the holder, and scatter the rose petals around the candle. Put the strawberries into a dish, and liberally drizzle honey all over them. Light the red candle, and think of your lover. Whisper their name to the flame of the candle. Eat one of the strawberries. Save the other to feed to your lover within 8 hours, or leave it by the ocean or under a tree as an offering to spirit.

FRIENDSHIP CANDLE SPELL

Friends are blessings. They keep us sane when everyone else disappears. You may be looking for a work buddy to share lunch with or a "ride or die" friend to keep all your secrets. Do this spell on a Friday night to shine a beacon that will help you make a new friend or find your tribe.

You need:

White votive candle

Heat-safe holder

Vanilla oil

Rose quartz tumbled stone

Unakite tumbled stone

Rhodonite tumbled stone
Emerald green satin mojo bag

Anoint the white candle with vanilla oil, and place it in the holder. Arrange the three stones around the candle holder, and light the candle. Imagine (or list) things you would like to do with the friends you will meet. If you are able to visualize, picture yourself laughing, happy, and healthy, enjoying your favorite activities with your new companion(s). Allow the candle to burn itself down; if this takes more than one session, always relight it on a Friday night. Place the stones in the green satin mojo bag with the leftover candle wax. Anoint the mojo bag with the vanilla oil, and carry it with you to draw kindred spirits to you.

NEVER GO TO BED ANGRY:
CLEARING THE AIR CANDLE SPELL

Every couple has disagreements, but arguing in the home can cause negative vibes. This spell clears out harmful energies, opens constructive communications, and brings unity to your space and your romantic connection. It can also be used in places of education, business, and other gatherings where cooperation and harmony are desired.

You need:
White tealight
Heat-safe dish
¼ cup coarse sea salt

¼ cup sage
Mortar and pestle
Paper and pen

Pour the salt and sage into the mortar, and blend them together with the pestle. As you grind the mixture, allow any anger you are experiencing to be vented. Yell if you need to. Cry if you want to. Then pause, take some deep breaths, and meditate on whatever disagreement or conflict has disturbed your peace. Write down all that is hoped to be resolved on the paper. Note how the relationship could be mended. What is needed to heal the situation? Compassion? Patience? Understanding? Write it all down, place the dish on top of the paper, and fill it with the mixture of sea salt and sage. Place the tealight on top of the mixture, and light it. After the candle extinguishes itself, pour the leftover sea salt and sage mixture outside your front door to keep the anger and disagreement away from the home. You can also tie the mixture in a fabric square and hang it on the back of the door, along with any of the following crystals or herbs:

Crystals to Banish Negativity
Smoky quartz: Blocks pessimism and melancholy
Obsidian: Clears bad vibes and depression
Amethyst: Reduces anxiety and defines boundaries

Herbs to Dissolve Anger
Rosemary: Wards off evil and protects
Sage: Expels annoyance and unblocks communication
Himalayan pink salt: Cleanses and safeguards love

OUR EXCLUSIVE FIDELITY SPELL

Here is the best spell to do when your mate has cheated on you to ensure it doesn't happen again. Get all their things in a box and leave it outside. You must allow yourself to feel no guilt as you block their phone number and change the locks by candlelight.

YOU NEED:
Black chime or taper candle
Heat–safe holder
Letter opener or other implement for carving
Mirror

To strengthen your resolve—so you don't let the same jerk back into your life—look into the mirror and tell yourself you are better than this and deserve more, much more. Engrave the name of the person who has harmed you into the black candle, set it firmly into the holder, and light it, saying, "You have broken my heart, and now we shall part." Let it burn to its entirety, along with the last fuck you have to give about the situation. Walk away and never look back.

The message here is simple: no candle can prevent a cheater from cheating. Save your energy for someone who will respect you and the boundaries of your commitment.

OUR FURRY, FEATHERED, OR SCALY FRIENDS: CONNECTING WITH YOUR FAMILIAR

Humans and their animal companions share an intense love and connection. Our pets become members of the family and love us unconditionally in a way people rarely ever do. Our "fur kids" are our truest friends and confidants. These sweet creatures hear and see it all. They appreciate and understand us better than we may even know ourselves.

A VINTAGE CANDLEHOLDER AND FAMILIAR MOJO BAG

Many Witches develop a bond with an animal that goes beyond the norm, and these animals are known as "familiars." Familiars are considered spirit guides who have taken the form of an animal on Earth. They are like soul mates with fur (or feathers, fins, or wings), imparting wisdom and acting as guards and guides in this world and beyond.

You need:
> Brown chime, taper, or votive candle
> Heat-safe holder
> Letter opener or other pointed implement for carving
> Rosemary oil
> Vanilla oil
> Photo of your pet
> Tumbled tiger's-eye
> Tumbled labradorite
> Gift from the animal (shed hair, claw sheath, or whisker; discarded feathers, shed skin, or similar)
> Brown satin mojo bag

On a Monday night during the waxing moon, or on a full moon any day of the week, carve the pet's name into the candle. Anoint the candle with rosemary oil first for protection. Next, rub the candle with vanilla oil to create the loving bond. Place the candle in its holder next to your pet's photo, and place the crystals on either side of it with the gift from the animal. Light the candle, repeat your pet's name nine times, and say the following:

"Faithful friend, my kith and kin,
Of feather, fur, or fang, or fin,

I welcome you into my pack.
I count on you to have my back.
I vow that I will care for you,
As long as you're my tried and true.
Be now and always at my side,
My steadfast guard and faithful guide."

Burn the candle until it extinguishes itself. Save the melted wax, gift from the pet, and crystals in the brown satin mojo bag tucked into your pillow. Keep the bag with you when you must travel away from your pet.

BREAKING TIES:
A RITE TO SEVER A BOND CANDLE SPELL

To release the past, you must fully embrace the present and realize that any attempts to bring the past into the present will cause discord and stress. Cutting ties with someone who has been in your life means removing all physical, mental, and spiritual bonds—and these three things are linked, so it is important to address them all.

First, return any belongings, because physical items contain the energy of the owner. Sell, donate, or toss anything that was given to you that will constantly bring up memories. If there is an item you got as a gift you cannot bear to part with and believe that in time you will not be pained by seeing it, tuck it away in a safe place while you do what it takes to get to that point.

The mental and spiritual work goes hand in hand. To formalize your intent to cut ties for good, you can perform a simple rite.

You need:
Heat-safe bowl
Small white candle in a heat-safe holder
Bay leaf
Pen

Write the person's name on the bay leaf. Hold it in your hand, and concentrate on the reasons why the relationship cannot continue. As each reason comes to you, release it by saying, "For this and other reasons, I am unbound." Repeat this as many times as there are reasons.

Light the white candle and set the leaf on fire with its flame. Do not attempt to hold onto the burning leaf; drop it into the bowl and watch it burn.

Recite the following:

"When these ashes hit the ground,
No trace of you with me is found.
I cut you loose to set me free,
Our ties are severed permanently.
As I do will, so mote it be."

Let the candle burn all the way down and dispose of any remnants. When the ashes of the leaf cool, take them outside and scatter them into the wind, watching as they blow away.

CHAPTER 4

FIERY WALL OF PROTECTION:
Banish the Bad Stuff

Every day, we encounter and open ourselves to the vibrations of nature, spirit, and the Universe. But many people don't realize the impact these forces have on their lives—unintentional negative energy can be absorbed from a person, place, or even an object. Have you ever been in a room with cigarette smokers, only to find later that your clothes and hair picked up the residue? Energy is like that. It's clingy, and it can be toxic.

When we ignore negative energies, their effects can become cumulative, with the potential to adversely affect everything and everyone close by. We all know how one person's bad mood can sour everyone else around them. In most cases, this is a passive impact. But what about when negativity is intentionally directed at you?

If you sense that envy or hate has been thrown your way, it is time to take action. Protection is self-preservation, and self-defense is one of the most innate instincts in the human psyche, going right down to the fight-or-flight core response every living creature on this planet possesses. Whether you encounter these energies from passive or active interactions, it is up to you to protect yourself. You can neutralize, deflect, or redirect the unwanted and harmful energies to safeguard not only yourself but those you love as well. Candle magic is a tried-and-true way of enforcing your boundaries and building a defensive barrier around your family, friends, property, body, mind, and soul.

WHEN DO YOU NEED PROTECTION?

The short answer is *always*. There is never a time when it's wise to leave the door open to opportunistic or random assaults. We have counseled clients about four categories of attacks.

ENEMIES AND FRENEMIES: PLANNED STRIKES

This is the most obvious time to reach for the candles. The reasons why people wish others harm are unlimited. They can be as simple as resentment and jealousy or even self-loathing, because as we've all learned in life, misery does indeed love company.

These intentional assaults seek to bring emotional damage, battering self-confidence to a point that the target is weakened. When a person feels powerless, their trust in their surroundings, and the people in it, diminishes. This is a key tool of perpetrators in abusive relationships, and we encounter far too many people who seek us out because they've found themselves in this unfortunate situation.

When a person is under energetic attack, they can feel depressed, anxious, exhausted, and agitated and suffer insomnia, nightmares, and other physical ailments. This state will compromise a person's emotional and physical health and should be considered a red alert to seek not only magical solutions but other forms of help as well. (Your doctor or local social services should be able to provide a list of resources, or you can call NAMI [the National Alliance on Mental Illness] at 800-950-NAMI from 10:00 a.m. to 8:00 p.m. ET, or text NAMI to 741741 for 24/7 confidential, free crisis counseling.)

LIFE LEECHES: ENERGY VAMPIRES

"It's not personal." How many times have you heard that and thought to yourself, *Well, it sure feels like it is?* With energy vampires, it may feel like the situation is about you, but it's not. It's about them, and you are caught in their trap, suffering collateral damage.

What is an energy vampire? Instead of draining their victims of blood, these thirsty takers absorb the energy and spirit of their victims. They are notoriously difficult to recognize, often charming their way into your life, appearing harmless or even weak. Some are easier to spot, appearing arrogant, boastful, or even smarmy. These psychic vampires are complainers, whiners, and users who do nothing to change their world but want to take time, energy, and sometimes money from their victims. Before you know it, you're staring into a bottomless pit of need.

If you notice that you always feel drained after dealing with a particular person, you need to extricate yourself from their web. Standing your ground and guarding your own energy is always the best medicine. Know that you are stronger and can overcome, no matter how many attempts you may need to get there. Cut the cords of attachment with confidence—and candle magic.

ACCIDENTAL ATTACKS

Unintentional forms of psychic attacks can happen when you least expect them. That is why practicing protection is so crucial. Many people come to us when they believe they have been cursed, but most of the time, it is simply a matter of being caught in the crossfire of someone else's bad day. This is not a case where someone has it out for you. It's more like being cut off in traffic, then having someone cut in front of you in line at the grocery store, and then finding that your car won't start.

Accidental attacks can also happen when someone physically or emotionally close to you is having a rough time. This energy can appear as if it was directed at you, or they may even take their frustration out on you without realizing they are doing it. In both of these cases, candle magic can wipe the slate clean and facilitate a fresh outlook for all involved.

FRIENDLY FIRE

Some of us attack ourselves unintentionally, letting our own negative thinking get the better of us. Self-doubt is the real enemy here, and it can become a self-fulfilling prophesy. A lack of confidence often breeds a lack of effort, which results in failure. Rarely does the person comprehend the source of the issue without guidance. Many of our clients believe they have been attacked from the outside, and delivering the truth can be a tough conversation.

Self-talk is magic. Treat it that way. Your mind is *the* most important tool you have for the best life possible. If you recognize yourself in the previous paragraph, it's up to you to catch yourself in the act of negative self-talk and change the soundtrack. If you hear yourself using "I can't" when pondering your goals, challenge yourself to reframe your point of view. "I haven't learned how to do this yet, but I am willing to make an effort" is a perfect place to start. Banish insults from your inner monologue. When you light your candles, believe in the magic that is *you*.

THE ELEMENTS OF YOUR OWN PROTECTION PRACTICE

Fire: Lighting a candle is the best way to invoke the protective aspects of Fire indoors. Carry a red candle through your space, walking counterclockwise, and banish the darkness of negativity with the light and heat of the flame.

Water: Burn a blue candle to invoke the cleansing virtue of Water while taking a shower or bath in the evening, and wash away any negative energy that has accumulated throughout the day. Lavender is both calming and cleansing, so you can use lavender soap and anoint the candle with lavender oil. Toss a bit of sea salt into the laundry with your clothes or linens to remove residual energy.

Air: To invoke the clarifying power of Air, light a yellow candle and some incense; we recommend frankincense and myrrh. Your personal practice may also include sage, palo santo, or other ingredients used to cleanse and sanctify a space. You can use sound to clear a space as well. Singing bowls, bells, or drums help change the vibration, or you can just turn on your favorite music and dance out those bad vibes. If it makes sense, open the windows to allow fresh air into the space. You may also choose to invoke Air's protection by speaking your intention from the heart.

Earth: Start by lighting a green candle to invoke the shielding force of Earth, and sweep from the front of your house to the back and right out the door. You can gently move the energy or really get down and sweep out the dirt. Place crystals of your choice in the four directions of your home, room, or place of business. Black tourmaline is a good choice; it is protective and absorbs any negativity in the area. (See the Table of Correspondences on page 220 for a complete list.) Eat a healthy meal of fresh food to ground and center you in your sanctuary.

Spirit: Surround yourself with friends you trust. These are your ride-or-die people. Nurture relationships based on honest communications, respect, and love.

WARDING YOUR HOME

Both of us cleanse our houses magically as well as mundanely—and frequently simultaneously. Leanne burns a black candle and lavender incense to banish negative energy and then calls on her ancestors to eliminate any bad vibes. She maintains a relationship with the good spirits within her house, asking for their aid in protecting the home. She also makes frequent offerings to her matron goddess Diana, asking that Her blessings be upon family and friends. Sandra stocks products that are formulated with herbs, essential oils, and all-natural ingredients that can do double duty, cleaning the surfaces and clearing the energy of her home. She has befriended the spirits of Gallows Hill since she was a child; her family has always taken care of the neighborhood in many ways and the resident souls keep careful watch over her—particularly her beloved grandfather, who in his living years was a Salem police officer who once walked a beat. Now that's some security!

It's simple to incorporate working with candles for protection into your life. After you've formed the habit, you'll find navigating your days much easier without the negativity of life weighing you down. Warding your space doesn't guarantee that nothing bad will happen, but it alerts you to the presence of unwanted energy so you can deal with it swiftly, and it lets negativity know it is not welcome there.

FOUR GUARDIANS CANDLE SPELL

After a particularly bad fight with an ex-friend, Leanne started experiencing mishaps and negativity in her home. She burned four black candles and placed iron railroad spikes in the four corners of her property to protect herself and her family. You don't have to do this reactively, after a relationship or situation has already gone south; it's an effective way to proactively protect your property and your peace of mind.

You need:
    4 black pillar candles
    4 heat-safe holders
    4 iron nail crosses or railroad spikes (symbol of protection)
    Compass or compass app on your phone

Use the compass to determine where the four directions fall on your property or in your space.

Starting in the east, place a black pillar candle in a holder and light it. Pass one symbol of protection over the fire. Allow the light and heat of the flame to imbue the symbol with energy. Say the following:

"Watchtower Guard,
   Protect me and mine.
   Stand vigil and shield
   Where rests this blest sign."

Repeat in the south, in the west, and finally in the north, lighting the candles and speaking the words of power. Take time with each candle, and let them extinguish themselves. (Note: place the candles in the area of the direction where they will not be disturbed, and if outdoors, use a hurricane glass or a jar candle to protect the flame from the wind. You may also choose to leave any remaining wax from each candle with the symbol of protection.) Place the symbol of protection somewhere it will not be disturbed. Outdoors, it should be buried in the earth. Indoors, it can be placed above doors or windows, hidden under floorboards, or similarly tucked away from the curious.

HOLD THE DOOR

Light a red candle on the right side of the door and a black candle on the left side, and let them burn for one hour. This can be done daily during times of trouble, and weekly or monthly otherwise to keep the spell strong.

Tie a small bundle of rowan twigs or pine needles with red cotton or wool thread and hang it on the back of the door as a protective talisman.

Place oak branches above the door, or acorns around it (inside is best), to stop ill from crossing into your home.

SHIELD CANDLE SPELL

A personal psychic shield should be your first line of defense, especially if you are going to do psychic work. (We are always surprised when we hear psychics say they do not make this part of their daily practice.) Learning to establish this armor can take some effort, but in time, it can become an instinctive way to protect yourself in a moment's notice.

You need:
> White candle
> Heat-safe holder
> Frankincense oil
> Statue or photograph of your chosen higher power

Find a quiet place to sit undisturbed. Take three deep breaths. Anoint the candle with frankincense oil, place it in the holder, and light it. Focus on the light of the candle as it blankets the statue or photo, and you, in its light. Repeat aloud several times:

> "*From your grace,*
> *Protect my body and space.*"

Imagine a web of this candlelight, like a protective net around you, shielding you from all harmful energy while still allowing good to enter. Try different visuals until you find one that feels right, keeping in mind that the shield should filter energy rather than totally block it. Sit in mindful meditation until you can visualize or feel the shield completely around you, imparting a feeling of safety and security. Snuff the candle, and reserve it for more shield work. If your skin is not sensitive to it, dab some frankincense oil on your wrists, and go and conquer the day.

FIERY WALL OF PROTECTION AND JOAN OF ARC LETTER OPENER

FIERY WALL OF PROTECTION CANDLE MEDITATION

This ritual is best performed monthly, whereas the protective barrier meditation can be used at any time. Carry the stones with you to draw on this barrier's strength whenever you're feeling exposed or scared.

You need:
> 5 red votive or pillar candles
> Heat-safe holders
> 5 stones: ruby, carnelian, red jasper, garnet, and/or fire agate
> Black charm bag
> Letter opener or other pointed implement for carving
>> (Leanne uses a special Yule gift from Sandra to carve all her protection and confidence candles: an antique brass Joan of Arc letter opener. This gives her the courage to say, "I am not afraid.")
> Optional: rattle

Sit comfortably in front of the altar or table where you will set up the candles. Begin by carving the name of the person/place in need of protection into each of the candles. Set the candleholders up in a row, like a wall, and securely insert the carved candles. Light each wick, from left to right. One by one, carefully pass each stone over the flame—not too close—and set each stone in front of a candle, from left to right.

As you watch the five flames dance, speak your desire aloud from your heart to the spirit of elemental Fire. Visualize a barricade materializing around what you want protected. Some people imagine angels surrounding them with shields; others see a wall of fire. Remain seated and raise energy by shaking a rattle, or if you are moved to do so, get up and raise energy by dancing like the flames.

When the meditation feels complete, let the candles burn for another hour before snuffing and reserving them to repeat every Tuesday night until the candles have burned down completely. Place the stones and leftover wax in the black charm bag, and carry as a talisman for protection.

A STREGA HERB JAR FOR PROTECTION

STREGA HERB JAR FOR PROTECTION CANDLE SPELL

Strega is Italian for "Witch" and has come to signify the practice of Italian folk magic. The canning jar commonly seen in old world Italian kitchens is as aesthetically pleasing as it is powerful. Every family has its own folk recipes, and this one is Leanne's.

You need:
Red taper candle (not dripless)
Black taper candle (not dripless)
Candle adhesive
Sea salt
Small mirrors
Iron shavings
Rue
Garlic (cloves, powder, or salt)
Bay leaves

¼ cup white vinegar
Canning jar with lid
Red ribbon

Place candle adhesive on the bottom of the red candle, and set it in the open canning jar. As you light the wick, envision a fortress around your home. Let the candle burn down completely, allowing the red wax to pool in the bottom of the jar and cool to a solid state. Pour ¼ cup of white vinegar in the jar over the red wax. Add in small amounts the sea salt, mirrors, iron shavings, rue, garlic, and bay leaves, just enough to create layers. When the jar is full, seal with the lid. Place candle adhesive on the bottom of the black candle and secure it to the top of the jar. Light the candle and allow the wax to drip down, eventually sealing the jar. When the wax is cool and hardened, tie a red ribbon around the lip of the jar, and place it in a window or near the entrance of the space that needs to be protected.

ANGELIC PROTECTION

Archangel Michael is known as the "great captain" of Heaven's army against evil. The name *Michael* means "one who is like God." He is a formidable friend when it comes to armor and protection magic, and he even appeared once as a column of fire to save a church from danger. Patron of firefighters, police officers, and armed service men and women, St. Michael can be called upon to protect you and give you courage, stamina, and strength, particularly in times of danger.

Sandra has been crafting her Gallows Hill Witchery St. Michael's Blessing talismans for nearly a decade. She has a carving of Archangel Michael that hangs on the wall by her bedroom door and an image of him in her car as well.

A CANDLE FOR ST. MICHAEL

Sandra and Leanne have both called upon Archangel Michael in times of trouble. Here is their candle spell to request his aid.

You need:
> 7-day St. Michael candle or red 7-day candle
> Bowl
> 1 cup clean water
> Image of St. Michael
> 4×4-inch piece of parchment paper
> Pen
> Lavender
> Thyme
> Red flowers
> Fire-safe container or cauldron

Set up a table either in a bedroom or by the entrance. Place the image of St. Michael on the table, with the flowers to the right. Fill the bowl halfway with water, and place it to the left. Write down on the parchment paper what is threatening and harming you. Place the paper in front of St. Michael on the table, and sprinkle the thyme and lavender on the paper. Light the candle. Ask St. Michael to give you guidance and protection.

Speak from the heart, or you may recite St. Michael's Prayer out loud:

"*St. Michael the Archangel,*
Defend us in battle,
Be our protection against the wickedness and snares of the devil.
May God rebuke him, we humbly pray.
And do thou, O Prince of the heavenly host,
By the power of God, cast into hell
Satan and all the evil spirits
Who prowl through the world seeking the ruin of souls.
Amen."

Collect the paper with the lavender and thyme, burn it in a fire-safe container, and bury the ashes.

STOP GOSSIP—STFU CANDLE SPELL

Gossip is harmful and creates an energy of mistrust and anxiety. Once trust has been violated in a relationship, the victim is left feeling betrayed and may struggle to let anyone in for a long time. Harmful trash talk can ruin friendships, alienate family members, and damage workplace morale.

You need:
    Black taper candle
    Heat-safe holder
    Letter opener or other pointed implement for carving

3 tablespoons cloves
3 tablespoons salt
Mortar and pestle
Olive oil
Dish

This is best done on a Saturday during the waning moon, or any time it is necessary. Pour the salt and cloves into the mortar and grind them with the pestle. While grinding, visualize the "trash talker's" mouth slamming shut, crushing their hurtful words right before they emerge. Grind until both ingredients are pulverized and you feel satisfied with the results. Pour the mixture into a dish.

If you know the names of the gossipers, carve them into the black candle and anoint it with olive oil. Deliberately and intentionally, work the oil into the candle. Roll the oiled candle in the salt-and-clove mixture. Place it securely in the holder, and light it. Name out loud each person who has spoken against you, and after each name, say the following:

"I crush your words.
May you taste their rot in your mouth."

Burn the candle down until it is gone. Take the remaining wax and toss it into the trash near the gossipers. If the gossipers are keyboard warriors who do not live anywhere near you (as is common in this time), toss the wax into the trash with a printout of their social media page or a slip of paper with their name/online persona on it.

WHEN ALL ELSE FAILS, RETURN TO SENDER CANDLE SPELL

Do no harm,
but take no shit.

—UNKNOWN

When you have tried all of the above and someone is still coming for you, the gloves gotta come off. This spell traps the offending party with their own negative energy, reflecting it back to them. Sometimes a taste of their own medicine is just what the doctor ordered.

You need:
> Black votive candle
> Heat-safe holder
> Letter opener or other pointed implement for carving
> 4 mirrors that can stand up, or 2 folding mirrors
> Olive oil
> Hot pepper flakes
> Tabasco sauce
> Photo of or writing sample from enemy
> Plastic bag

Carve the name(s) of your target(s) into the black candle. Coat with olive oil, roll in red pepper flakes, and place securely in the holder. Drizzle the candle with Tabasco sauce, avoiding the wick. Light the candle and surround it with the mirrors. Allow the candle to burn all the way down. Stick the remaining wax and the photo or writing sample into a plastic bag, and toss it into the bottom of your freezer.

CHAPTER 5

KEEPING THE LIGHTS ON:
Career Concerns and Money Mojo

M any of our clients are unhappy with their financial situations and are desperate for their savings to grow. Bills consume so much of so many hard-working folks' income, they never get to put their money toward fun things like travel or making nonmaterial improvements in their lives. Not having control over one's economic stability is disheartening. Everyone wants more.

Money is second only to love as the topic people want to hear about in our readings, and supplies for money magic fly off the shelves in our shops. Candles are at the top of that list.

Candle magic can indeed help manifest career creativity and inspiration, leading to increases in both satisfaction and income. As always, change comes through action. Fire's dual nature of destruction and creation can help you take control of your wallet and your life. Focusing your mind on the power of Fire, debt can be turned to ash, and from those ashes, opportunity, prosperity, and abundance rise.

THE SMELL OF MONEY: AROMATHERAPY FOR YOUR WALLET

Aromatherapy has been around for thousands of years, and in more recent times has gained recognition from Western medicine. But the potency of scent is not limited to healing the body or the mind. You can put it to use to mend your broken budget and invite in wealth, too.

Certain scents have long been thought to attract money, protect what you have earned, and bring career blessings. To employ their power, you can either dress an unscented candle in an oil or purchase a candle with the essence already infused. (We're not above going to the Dollar Store for scented candles. Leanne's favorite is apple cinnamon, a double whammy when lit that draws both love and money into her home.)

PERFUMES OF PROSPERITY

These are our go-to scents to bring abundance into your life:

Honeysuckle: Sweet and rich—what's not to like? This delicious aroma will attract money to you like bees to honey. It boosts self-confidence, which helps in job interviews or when you are negotiating employment benefits or a raise. It is associated with fortune and bounty and attracts these blessings into a home or business. Sandra has a honeysuckle room spray that she keeps in her front hall and deploys often to encourage wealth to enter her home; it is the last thing she smells before she sets out to tackle the day. **Begin a honeysuckle candle on a Sunday to draw quick cash, or on a Thursday to influence employers.**

Pine: A strong scent filled with vitality, mighty pine will protect your wallet from overspending, particularly helpful around the holidays and during extended bouts of retail therapy. **Begin a pine candle on a Saturday to invoke Saturn's affinity for boundaries to help you stop adding to your cart and start sticking to your budget.**

Cedar: Another woodsy note, cedar protects what you have already and gives you the strength and wisdom to keep your finances strong. The idea of preservation has been linked with this pleasant scent for hundreds of years as the primary material of the hope chest (once called a "dowry chest"), a holdover from the days when a bride entered a marriage with valuables and property, and the cedar kept linens and other fabric items safe from insects and mold. Cedars are evergreens, and in the United States, our money is green, so "ever green" has an added layer of meaning. **Start a cedar candle on a Tuesday to strengthen your financial armor.**

Grapefruit: Nothing says "Good morning" like the scent of grapefruit blessing your day and your bank account. Like other citrus scents, it is associated with the sun, which is responsible for all growing things. **Grow your savings by lighting a grapefruit candle on a Sunday and making a plan to put away a little bit from each paycheck into a rainy-day fund for those times when the sun hides.**

Lemon: This zesty scent energizes your wallet with confidence and new beginnings. **Clean or dust your home with lemon-scented cleanser and follow it up with a lemon candle on a Sunday to invoke that "clean slate" vibe and turn over a new financial leaf.** You can create your own cleanser with lemon peels and white vinegar: soak the rinds in the vinegar for a week, and you've got a great homemade cleaner to take your aromatherapy candle magic to the next level.

Orange: The last of our citrus trio, optimistic orange warms with the sun's power for prosperity and growth. The color orange is associated with Mercury, the fastest-traveling planet in our solar system, so it helps speed up things. **Combine the forces of the sun and Mercury to give your finances a quick dose of luck by burning an orange candle anointed or scented with orange oil.** For fast cash, light it on a Sunday. For a rapid response to a job application, light it on a Wednesday. And in a financial emergency, light it ASAP.

Cinnamon: Cinnamon is one of the most versatile spell ingredients we know. It has been associated with everything from love, luck, and success to health and protection, but one of its most popular uses is to grow wealth. It is also one of the easiest herbs to layer to increase its magical effectiveness because you can put it in a beverage or on your food, write a wish on paper and wrap it around a cinnamon stick to tuck into your pillowcase or carry with you, and of course, anoint candles with cinnamon oil and burn them. **Light a cinnamon candle on a Friday to form alliances and develop relationships with financially stable business or life partners.**

Nutmeg: Nutmeg comes from a tropical evergreen tree, and the spice has been used to flavor all kinds of foods (main courses as well as desserts) and beverages (like eggnog!), so this is another scent you can layer to increase its impact. You may even decide to really spice things up and make a sachet to place in the drawer with your underthings. Just don't overdo it if you choose to ingest it because it can be dangerous in high doses. The safest way to work with nutmeg is to get a nutmeg-scented candle. Gamblers sometimes carry a whole nutmeg with them to increase their likelihood of winning cash during games of chance, and you can carry one with a piece of devil's shoestring to a job interview to have luck on your side. **Burn a nutmeg candle before an interview to increase the odds you'll be hired or before you hit the casino to invite Lady Luck to your table.**

Cloves: From yet another evergreen (are you seeing a pattern?), this one tropical like nutmeg, these dried buds are ruled by the planet Jupiter, which is associated with long-term wealth, status, influence, and power—even royalty. Clove buds can be pushed directly into the sides of a candle or placed to form shapes or accent carvings of symbols, dates, or other information pertinent to the spell. Pregnant women and people with sensitive stomachs should avoid ingesting it, but the scent itself should not cause issues. **Burn a clove candle on a Thursday to support your long-term plans for success in business and financial security.**

Pumpkin pie: More spice, bigger slice. Here's a Witchy hack we've had success with: burning pumpkin pie candles to manifest bounty and make bank. This scent has everything you need, a mixture of cinnamon, nutmeg, and clove that makes for an unbeatable combination of money mojo. It smells delicious, too.

Cultivating gratitude for the blessings already in your life is essential to obtaining more. Continually asking the Universe for more and never saying thank you for what you already have is an insult to the Divine. Start your day with gratitude and love. Pause and take time to create a relationship with the energy that created the world around you. It isn't always easy to see the splendor and joy when life is difficult, but pick one gift and be grateful for it. When you approach your day from a place of thankfulness, you open yourself to more good fortune.

CANDLES FOR CAREER CONFIDENCE

In October 2020—during a global pandemic—Leanne opened Pentagram in Salem, Massachusetts, with Timothy Reagan. Her career was about to change dramatically. She didn't just need money; she needed the confidence to leave the safety of her career at Hex: Old World Witchery. This was an opportunity to prove to herself that she was capable of being a businesswoman, juggling her psychic career and her own store. It happened rapidly: two months from an advertisement of an open location to an agreement. Just eight weeks to build the store from the ground up in time to open the doors on the first day of the busiest month of the year. There was no time for self-doubt.

Leanne turned to the element of Fire for the help she needed. She worked with a yellow beeswax 7-day candle—a gift from Sandra for her birthday that July—dressed in lemon oil. Burning it on Sunday, first thanking the powers that be for the career and gifts that brought her this prospect, she lit the wick to bring a mighty force of self-reliance to her soul. Spells like these are both deceivingly simple and remarkably effective. Here are some you can put to work in your life.

A FIRE TO INSPIRE: SUCCESS CANDLE SPELL

This spell is designed to be a catalyst. This fire heralds the change you have been hoping for.

You need:

> Yellow or gold candle
> Basil oil (or olive oil and dried basil)
> Letter opener or other pointed implement for carving
> Heat-safe holder

This spell is best begun on a Sunday, but any day when inspiration strikes is a good time to start. After all, that's the whole point. Engrave your initials and an image of the sun on a gold or yellow candle. You can rub basil oil on the candle to bring abundance and protect the wealth you create. As you are infusing the wax with the oil, envision yourself succeeding in your goals and projects. (If you are unable to visualize this, you can write down your desires on paper just before you touch the candle.) Imagine a positive force surrounding you, supporting your hopes and dreams. Place the candle in the holder, and as you light it, note the light and warmth that is generated.

Speak these words:

"I light this candle on this day,
And all self-doubt is burned away.
Nothing here can hold me down,
No one can keep me from my crown.
I carry this flame within my heart,
Its light will guide the course I chart.
My hopes and dreams will come to me,
As I do will, so shall it be."

Allow the candle to burn for at least 1 hour before snuffing it out. Repeat for 3 days or until the candle is completely consumed.

EASY COME AND DON'T GO:
MONEY WHEEL CANDLE SPELL

To gain more money and to activate your Midas touch, create a spell using nine candles.

You need:
> 9 tealight, votive, or taper candles: 1 royal blue, 4 gold or
> yellow, and 4 green
> 9 heat-safe holders

Place the four green candles in their holders on the table in the four directions: north, south, east, and west. Place the four yellow or gold candles in their holders between them in the northeast, southeast, southwest, and northwest. Place the royal blue candle in its holder directly in the center.

Light the center candle first and then start in the east and light the others, going around the circle clockwise until all candles are lit. (Be especially careful as you maneuver, and watch out for the candles that are already lit.)

As you light the candles, say this at least once for each:

"Money to hand, money to touch,
Money will come to me in a rush."

If you chose tealight candles, let them burn all the way down. If you chose votives or tapers, you can snuff them and work with them two more times or until they burn down completely.

BIG WALLET ENERGY CANDLE SPELL ENVELOPE

MAJOR PURCHASING POWER:
BIG WALLET ENERGY CANDLE SPELL

Life is expensive, but it is worth every penny. If you are looking to make a major purchase, such as a car, a new home, or a business, put this spell to work for you.

You need:
Green taper candle
Heat-safe candle holder
Letter opener or other pointed implement for carving
2 tablespoons patchouli
2 tablespoons basil
Bay leaf

About 1 yard twine

Pyrite

Photo or sketch of your target

Envelope

Put the rendering of your desired purchase into the envelope, and tuck in the herbs. Seal the envelope and place pyrite on top. In the green taper candle, carve a star with one point at the bottom and two points at the top. Place the taper in the holder and light the wick. When the wax starts to build up, carefully pick up the candle and drip some wax on the envelope's flap to seal the point. Place the candle back into the holder. When the wax dries, wrap the twine around the envelope three times. As you tie it in a knot, say these words four times:

"Sealed with wax and tied with twine,
What I want will be all mine."

Continue to burn the candle until it is completely gone. After the wax on the envelope is completely cooled, place the envelope in your pillowcase along with the pyrite. You can carry the pyrite with you each day to keep the spell active. When it comes time to purchase the object of your desire, bring the envelope with you, keeping it in a pocket or purse out of sight.

JUPITER, LIGHT THE WAY!: CAREER GUIDANCE CANDLE SPELL

Looking to start a new project or business, or learn something new to generate income? Try this candle spell.

You need:

Royal blue or royal purple taper or tall, thin pillar candle

Orange oil

Rosemary oil

Letter opener or other pointed implement for carving

Heat-safe bowl

1 cup clean water

Thursday is the day to seek guidance for long-range plans and win the support of people in high places. Jump-start these ventures by beginning your work at sunrise. After all, the early bird catches the worm. The combination of water (to increase your intuition) and fire (to shed light on the best path) brings you the wisdom to make the right choices to achieve your goals.

Slowly pour the water into the bowl. As you do this, think about what questions you want answered about your path. Take a few moments to consider what words could sum up your goals and then engrave them into the candle. Dress your candle with a drop of orange oil and a drop of rosemary oil to extend the potency of your spell. Light the candle, and pay attention to the shadows of the flame. See what shapes speak to you. Messages from the shapes of shadows can direct you on what steps to take before you begin your new endeavor. You can read both the flickering of the flames and the wax that forms from the burning of the candle. (See Chapter 11 for detailed instructions on both.)

As you snuff out the candle, give thanks for the wisdom you have been given.

YOUR TIME TO SHINE: OPPORTUNITY CANDLE SPELL

Is there a particular job you are hoping to land? Is there a position in your current place of employment you want to move into?

You need:
  Yellow votive or pillar candle
  Royal blue votive or pillar candle
  Job advertisement or description on paper
  2×3-inch gold or blue charm bag
  Letter opener or other pointed implement for carving
  1 piece devil's shoestring
  Heat-safe bowl
  1 cup clean water

Print a copy of the job advertisement or write out the job description you desire. Take three deep breaths, inhaling through your nose and exhaling through your mouth. Picture yourself at the interview. Hear your own voice professionally impressing the interviewer. Then imagine yourself on a typical day in that position. Envision yourself succeeding. (As an alternative to visualization, you can write out your desired scenario on paper.) When you have framed your goal, slip the paper containing the job ad or your desires under the bowl and create the spell candles.

Start with the yellow candle. Engrave it with your name followed by the job title you want while focusing on the feeling of success. As you carve the yellow candle, repeat six times, "Opportunity flows.

Opportunity grows." Pour the water into the bowl, and as you pour, repeat the words again six times. Place the yellow candle in the bowl, and light it, repeating the words again six times as the wick ignites.

Engrave the royal blue candle with the job title and the name of the company you are hoping to work for. As you start carving into the wax, repeat four times, "I shine. This job is mine." Place the blue candle next to the yellow candle in the bowl, and light it, repeating the words again four times.

Place the piece of devil's shoestring in the water.

Burn these candles for at least 1 hour each day until they are extinguished. Place any leftover wax in a gold or blue charm bag with the piece of devil's shoestring as a beacon for success. Tuck it into your pillowcase when you sleep, and carry it with you during the day.

DEBT REDUCTION CANDLE SPELL

Sometimes we wake up with the smell of money in the air. The day begins with the energy and enough drive to conquer the world. Other days are not so great. Schedules are jam-packed, emotions are overwhelming, and we just want some retail therapy. Meanwhile, our bank accounts just need a break. If you're in over your head, here's how you can begin to remedy the situation.

You need:
> Gold or green taper candle
> Black taper candle
> ½ cup sea salt

2×3-inch green charm bag
2 heat-safe bowls

Divide the sea salt evenly between the bowls. Place the black candle in one bowl and the gold or green candle in the other. (If it seems like your sea salt is not enough to keep your candles upright, you can carefully use a lighter to warm the bottom of the candle, using the hot wax to adhere each candle to its bowl, and then add the salt. Alternatively, you may use candle adhesive if you have it handy.)

The black candle draws in and neutralizes the energy that generated the debt and the negativity that has been fueling your poor financial habits. As you light it, say out loud five times, "Debt is banished! Debt has vanished!"

The gold or green candle represents the prosperity that is flowing back into your bank account and your life. When you light it, repeat the following three times:

"Money, money, come my way,
Money troubles go away.
Money, money, here to stay,
More money than I need to pay."

Let the candles burn down as far as possible.

Toss the remnants of the black candle and the sea salt it was burning in into a river or ocean. If no running water is nearby, toss them into a trash receptacle somewhere away from your home or place of business.

Place the remnants of the gold candle and the sea salt it was burning in into the green charm bag. Carry this charm to draw money in and feel more in control of your finances.

PLANETARY CANDLE SPELLS TO BLESS YOUR BUSINESS

Every day at Pentagram, Leanne and her business partner light a candle in a glass container filled with water to receive planetary blessings. Leanne adds a pinch or two of agrimony to her business spells every day because it draws in not just money but also success.

On Sunday, they light a yellow candle with ground cinnamon and calendula petals in the water, which heightens their joyful spirits and monetary luck with the powerful shining spirit of the Sun. Sol, the Sun, grants growth and health to the shop and those who run and patronize it.

On Mondays, they burn a lilac candle with milk thistle or rose in the water to harness the intuitive powers of the moon. The gift of enhanced perception facilitates harmony and peaceful cooperation in the shop.

On Tuesdays, they burn a red candle with nettle or pepper in the water to obtain vigor, strength, and passion from the planet Mars. This protects the business from any and all dangers, including theft.

On Wednesdays, they burn an orange candle with meadowsweet or honeysuckle in the water to receive the gifts of clear communication and heightened intellect from the planet Mercury. This energy helps Leanne and Tim connect with each other and with clients and make smart business decisions without delay.

On Thursdays, it's a royal blue candle, with jasmine or comfrey in the water, which gains the recognition and admiration of prospective as well as current patrons and the blessings of the great planet Jupiter. This influence supports their store's reach and success.

On Fridays, they light a green candle with hibiscus or red raspberry leaf in the water to receive the blessing of the abundant spirit of Venus, planet of love and beauty. Venus grants richness and well-being to clients and employees alike.

On Saturdays, they burn a black candle with poppy or St. John's wort in the water to expel discord and negative influences from outside sources. The black candle draws in the blessing of the planet Saturn, which blocks negativity and facilitates spirit communication.

You can create a similar space in your own place of business to focus on drawing in blessings for success and prosperity. It doesn't have to be elaborate, especially when you begin. Keep it simple. Create a dedicated area to safely light a candle each day before you open for business. Take a few moments to focus on creating the atmosphere you want for yourself and your customers. Begin each workday with a positive mind-set and a spotlight on your mission, and watch your business—and your satisfaction—grow.

CHAPTER 6

YOUR GLOW UP:
Ignite Health and Well-Being

Aside from the candles we light on the main altar and in the four quarters for our rituals, the most common reason we light candles is healing. Looking back over all the magic we have done through the years, there is no greater need, no more urgent desire, than someone's health. As the saying goes, "When you have your health, you have everything. When you do not have your health, nothing else matters at all." This statement is attributed to Augusten Burroughs, but it has been paraphrased by many others because it's a timeless truth.

Candles can be used for healing on all levels: physical, emotional, mental, and spiritual. To exert the energy it takes to send healing to others, you must take care of yourself first. Maybe you're already bristling at that advice. In our work, we have learned that psychically active and sensitive people commonly put themselves last when it comes to care. This is a recipe for burnout. If you're going to work healing for others, you've got to ensure you have a good self-care practice in place first.

#SELFCARE 101 FOR #EMPATHS

You've probably noticed that both of these terms have become mammoth buzzwords. When the world feels dark and chaotic, they must go hand in hand. Self-care is an essential first step on the road to happiness and success for anyone, but it is particularly vital for those who have high levels of empathy and are influenced by the feelings of those around them.

Many people who are empathic carry a fierce desire to heal the people they love. But when we forget about our own spiritual, emotional, and physical journey, drawing the energy to help others is exhausting. Think of it this way: if you want to run an errand for someone you care about, it's not selfish to put fuel in your gas tank—it's necessary.

Love thyself.

Upon waking each morning, give gratitude. Start by thanking the Universe for the promise of a new day. Both of us have a morning practice. Leanne sits at her bed and expresses her thanks, both for protection while she and her family slept and for the opportunity to live another day. Sandra incorporates a stretch and sets her intention with one or two simple statements, such as "Today is going to be a good day. I'm going to work toward my goals and be gentle with myself."

No matter who we are or what we believe, we all share a common destination when we get out of bed: the bathroom. Our reflection in the mirror greets us, and it may not be the most flattering appearance. Then there is the scale, sometimes with numbers that are higher than we expected, which often glare at us as if to say, "I know what you did!" These are cues for negative self-talk, like "I'm so fat," "Ugh . . . bad hair day," or "I look old," which is not how anyone should begin their day. It's time to switch up the program.

The flame from a single candle can burn away what we no longer want or need in any space. Fire allows for peace of mind, body, and spirit for those willing to bathe in its light. Instead of jumping into the shower and pulling on whatever clothes are at hand, light a candle first and turn your morning routine into a sacred ritual. It doesn't have to be elaborate; in fact, the simpler, the better, because it needs to fit into your busy morning schedule.

MORNING MAGIC CANDLE SPELL

You'd be surprised at how much one candle can adjust your attitude. Try this for seven days, and note the way it changes your approach to, and your overall experience of, your day-to-day life.

You need:
  Pink or white taper candle
  Heat-safe holder
  3 drops bergamot oil
  Letter opener or other pointed implement for carving

Pink candles are perfect for those days when negative self-talk is particularly painful. Pink brings peace and emotional healing and opens you to self-love. If you don't have a pink candle, a white one will work, too. Carve your name into the candle and then rub in 3 drops of bergamot oil from the top to the bottom. As you prepare the candle, visualize the sun breaking through the clouds, clearing away the shadows of worry and self-doubt. Picture the sunlight on your face, warming you, restoring your self-worth and confidence. Place the candle in the holder, and as you light it, watch the flame grow, and with it, your sense of inner peace. Speak to the flame, something from the heart, or you may use these words:

"Fire of life, fire of love,
  Grant me divine strength from the Goddess above!"

If you choose to shower afterward, picture the water containing the same energy that emanates from the light of the candle. Either way, when you next look in the mirror, wish yourself a fantastic day. When you have finished getting ready, snuff out the candle and know that you are prepared to face whatever the day brings with strength and grace.

BATHED IN LIGHT CANDLE SPELL

There are days when you are feeling so uninspired that a quick shower and one candle will not be enough. In this case, make some time to soak in a sea salt bath. The salt will dissolve any negativity that's clinging on, and being immersed in water will naturally decrease both physical and mental pressure and increase your connection to the Divine. The combination of salt and water is both purifying and nourishing and washes away anxiety, tension, stress, and disquiet. The warm water also helps relax the mind so the magic of will and desire can expand outward into the Universe. This is an excellent way to prepare for any ritual or psychic work.

You need:

    3 tealights, votives, or small jar candles: 1 pink, 1 green, and 1 white (This color combination promotes self-love, confidence, good health, and a feeling of abundance. You can substitute with all white if you don't have the other colors.)

    3 heat-safe holders

    Safe, sturdy location in the bathroom to place the candles

    Optional: 1 piece rose quartz, 1 piece aventurine, and 1 clear quartz crystal

Draw a warm bath. As you light the white candle, visualize yourself bathed in purifying white light that cleanses away the worries of the day. If you are using stones in this spell, hold the clear quartz at the same time and then place it in the bathwater. Light the pink candle and imagine yourself bathed in warm pink light that feels like a caring hug. As you do so, pick up and hold the rose quartz and then place it in the bathwater. Finally, light the green candle and see yourself bathed in fertile green healing light, growing the positive energy raised by the pink light. Pick up and hold the aventurine while you do this part of the visualization and then place it in the bathwater.

After the candles are lit, climb into the bath and picture any remaining negative thoughts dissolving like the salt. When you feel your mood has lifted, extinguish the candles and drain the tub, imagining any and all negativity washing down the drain. If you used stones, gather them and carry them with you until the next new moon to maximize the effects of this spell.

Leanne remembers: *As a young child, I recall how my mother would light a soft blue candle on the bathroom countertop and sit perched on the edge of the tub as I played. I remember her helping dry me off and telling me I was cleaned by "the blessed mother." To this day, I light a candle when I soak in the tub and think of my connection to the Divine feminine. I ask for help to see the beauty within myself.*

EVERYDAY CANDLE MAGIC FOR WELL-BEING

Each of the days of the week is named for, and therefore linked with, one of what Witches call the Seven Sacred Planets. The influence of these planets forms the basis of horoscopes, and they can help you work on your health and well-being. Here are some suggestions to harness their unique energies and correspondences.

SUNDAY MORNING MOJO:
GROWING YOUR STRENGTH AND POWER

The sun is responsible for all living things on the planet and signifies growth, strength, determination, and leadership. Its impact on our health is scientifically proven, and its absence during the winter months is why many of us become depressed due to the shorter, darker days. In many faiths, the sun is linked with divinity, often the energy of the Creator, and associated with masculine deities. Where the sun is located in the sky at the time of your birth determines your zodiac sign. **Light a yellow or gold candle on a Sunday to facilitate new beginnings, and empower yourself with the might of the sun to make changes for better health.**

NOT JUST ANOTHER MANIC MONDAY:
PSYCHIC WELL-BEING

Monday is the day of the moon—a symbol of the Goddess. As it rules the tides on Earth, the moon holds sway over the element of Water, which is associated with intuition. Because water makes up the majority of the human body, this planet is extremely potent for both physical and emotional healing as well as metaphysical well-being. **To** activate psychic healing, burn a silver candle on a Monday to strengthen your intuitive gifts as well as your ability to send healing energy to others. This will also magnify lunar energies to manifest prophetic dreams and empower the Divine feminine within.

GOOD-BYE, RUBY TUESDAY:
TEMPER TRANSFORMATION

It's natural to feel angry when wronged, but what you do with those emotions can make all the difference. Feeling a bit fired up? Rage and stress have been scientifically linked to countless physical ailments, and holding on to anger weakens the body and the mind. That fiery energy can be transformed into something that will feed your efforts toward your objectives. Tuesday is the day of Mars, the planet of warfare and strategy, but it's also the planet of passion, and passion fuels our goals. **Burn a red candle on a Tuesday to meditate on whatever has upset and angered you, and ask for clarity and guidance to turn the conflict into a force that will help you move ahead in the areas you feel passionate about.**

WEDNESDAY MORNING:
HEALTHY COMMUNICATION AND SWIFT RECOVERY

Communication is key to building healthy relationships. Whether it's a relationship with someone else or with yourself, Wednesday is the perfect day to work on self-expression and communication because it is associated with Mercury, the messenger of the gods. **Light an orange candle on a Wednesday, envision orange light around your throat, hear your voice strongly and clearly stating your truth with compassion, and receive compassion in return.** Visualize the energy flowing, easily and swiftly, between all parties. This is also a good day to work on safely speeding up any healing process. In that case, imagine the area that requires healing, both physical and otherwise, surrounded in the orange light.

SWEET THURSDAY:
FIX YOUR CROWN, AND RULE YOUR CONSTITUTION

Thursday is devoted to Jupiter, the planet of expansion and great fortune, so this is the day to project for good luck when it comes to your health. Jupiter is named for the king of the gods, so invoke sovereignty over your well-being today. Jupiter holds sway over people of influence, including politicians, lawyers, and doctors. **If you are planning an important appointment, light a blue candle on a Thursday for positive influence and good news.**

IT'S FRIDAY, I'M IN LOVE:
EMOTIONAL VITALITY BOOSTER

The planet Venus, like the Goddess of the same name, rules beauty and love. Candles can illuminate a beauty you may not always see within the darkness of your own mind. **Light a pink candle on a**

Friday to invite in blessings of all kinds of love—self-love, friendship, romantic love, and the broader love of humanity—giving you a healthy dose of affection and appreciation.

SATURDAY NIGHT FEVER: BANISH NEGATIVITY AND ESTABLISH HEALTHY BOUNDARIES

Saturday is named for the planet Saturn, which governs study, responsibility, time, accountability, and defense. One of the colors we use to connect to Saturn's energy is black, which represents power, protection, and authority. **Burn a black candle on a Saturday to remove any negative thoughts or energies that have built up during the week and to safeguard your mental health.** You may also add a white candle to increase and preserve the positive gains you have made through the week. The color combination promotes unity, completeness, and balance.

Making candle-burning a regular practice continuously supports your health goals. In addition to your daily routine, there will be times when you have specific health concerns that would benefit from candle magic, including illnesses and injuries, planned procedures like surgeries, and pregnancy.

HEALTH EMERGENCIES

When you find out someone you care about is sick or has been injured, you wish there was something you could do to help. When you find out everyone on the planet is facing a global pandemic, this feeling is magnified exponentially! For decades, we have been doing candle magic whenever someone we loved was in distress, but we never expected to be doing that kind of healing work on a daily basis the way we were throughout 2020.

In the case of genuine health emergencies, a simple white candle of any kind is all that is needed to begin the spell. If you have a healing oil, such as eucalyptus, peppermint, lemon, clove, frankincense, sandalwood, or tea tree, you can anoint the candle with it. Frankincense is Sandra's go-to, and no matter how many other oils she layers on, that's where she begins when she prepares a candle for healing.

In any emergency, you don't need to wait for a specific day or phase of the moon or fuss with the materials or the wording. Speak from the heart. Say the person's name if you are sending medicine to a specific person. You can write it on a paper and slip it under the heat-safe candleholder if you wish. Specifically say that you are sending them healing energy for them to draw upon. Focus on the base of the flame, and visualize the light wave emanating out from the candle and surrounding the person (or people) with the salve they require. (Candle magic is, of course, done in conjunction with seeking medical attention, not as a substitute for it.)

PLANNED PROCEDURES

Whether it's your own surgery or that of someone you love, the days leading up to the procedure are filled with worry and dread. Stress is not conducive to healing, so practice deep breathing exercises and candle magic to reduce anxiety and promote peace of mind. Keep it simple so you don't add any pressure to your routine: **light a white tealight candle each night.** Choose a shallow tealight that burns for about three hours, and begin the spell three hours before bed to allow it to burn out. When you are ready to light the candle, do the following breathing exercise first to clear your mind: inhale through your nose for five seconds, hold that breath for five seconds, exhale through your mouth for five seconds, and wait five seconds before inhaling again. Count out each number in your mind. The idea is to focus fully and completely on your breath and nothing else. Repeat three to five times before lighting the candle. Envision yourself waking up pain-free and calm following your procedure. You can do the same when someone you care about is going to have an operation.

If you get the news that someone you love is about to undergo emergency surgery, it's likely you won't have time to gather specific materials. When it is a planned procedure, however, you may have time to procure a figure candle in their image. **A figure candle is particularly helpful when visualizing physical aid, and you can carve symbols into specific areas of the figure to target that healing.** You can anoint the candle with a healing oil (frankincense or a healing blend) and light it on the morning of the procedure. If possible, keep it burning until you hear the person is conscious again (as long as you don't have to leave it unattended). In the following days, continue to use the candle to support a smooth, swift recovery.

PREGNANCY

The foundation of fertility is health, and many cultures light a candle to promote well-being before, during, and after a pregnancy. Traditional pregnancy spells using candles are simple but powerful. Timing is important; it is best to do fertility magic on the new moon once it can be seen in the sky with the naked eye because that is the time of new beginnings. When trying to conceive her first child, Leanne lit a candle and left flowers at a statue of the Virgin Mother asking for her blessing. Three weeks later, Leanne was pregnant with her first child, Elizabeth.

FERTILITY CANDLE SPELL

Timing: Visible new moon

You need:
Green votive or pillar candle
3 drops soothing oil (lavender or sandalwood)
½ teaspoon citrus oil (orange, lemon, or grapefruit)
Heat-safe bowl
1 cup clean water
Letter opener or other pointed implement for carving

Pour about 1 inch of clean water into the bowl, and sprinkle it with one of the citrus oils. These oils correspond to the sun and its nurturing force of growth, joy, and overall positivity. Water symbolizes the womb and the source of life on our planet.

Carve the astrological symbol for Earth, an equal-arm cross inside a circle, into the side of the candle. It is appropriate here, not only because of the fertility of the Earth element and Earth itself but because the plus sign it resembles is commonly associated with a positive pregnancy test.

Rub 3 drops of the soothing oil on the candle from the top to the bottom, and visualize any nervousness or tension about getting pregnant melting away. This is a crucial part of the spell because the stress of trying to get pregnant can impact your chances to conceive.

Place the anointed candle in the bowl of water, and light it, saying the following:

> "Fire of life, water of the womb,
> Power of the sun to make things bloom,
> Help us grow our family,
> As we wish, so may it be."

As always, do not leave the burning candle unattended. You can snuff it out and relight it for 3 consecutive nights. Any remaining wax should be buried in the fertile earth.

SEEKING BETTER HEALTH
BY REACHING OPTIMAL BODY WEIGHT

Both of us have recently been on a weight-loss journey, and candle magic has figured prominently into it. On Mondays, Leanne summons the aid of her patron goddess to give her the strength to make healthy choices. She uses a silver or light purple candle and calls on the spirit of Artemis, lunar Goddess of the hunt. Artemis gives healing and strength to women and has been a presence in Leanne's life since she first acknowledged her devotion to the Divine feminine.

Sandra has set up an elaborate altar dedicated to healing, with statues of Hygeia and Apollo at the center, facing a candelabra that holds five tealights or votives. Those five candles symbolize a restoration of balance to all the factors that enter into her relationship with her body: one for her mind (element of Air), one for her strength of will/willpower (element of Fire), one for her physical condition (element of Earth), one for her heart/emotions (element of Water), one for her connection to the Divine (element of Spirit). As she ignites each candle, she visualizes the light energy being absorbed into her skin, imbuing her with renewed strength and restoring the balance among the elements.

You can do this as well. Line up five tealight candles in heat-safe holders, and as you kindle each one, visualize the light sinking into your skin. You may choose to speak an affirmation each time:

> "Light of Air, illuminate my mind, that I may create healthy habits
>   and make the best choices.
> Light of Fire, fuel my willpower, that I may steel myself against
>   temptations.
> Light of Earth, nourish my body, that I may increase my strength,
>   flexibility, and stamina.

Light of Water, fill my heart with compassion for myself, that I may quench my desire with love.
Light of Spirit, satisfy the desires of my soul, that I may reach my greatest potential."

We wish you all the brightest blessings on your own health journey.

CHAPTER 7

LIGHTING THE WAY BACK:
Breaking Bad Habits and Addictions

Addiction damages both an individual and the people who love them and forms a pattern of behavior that is detrimental to one's health and well-being. Living with an addiction is similar to going through life holding a ticking time bomb. The addict is always on edge, waiting for the shrapnel of depression, sickness, and disorder to blow apart everything worthwhile.

Addiction is commonly thought of as a dependency on substances, such as drugs or alcohol, but many people are addicted to behaviors that give them a kind of high. Certain behaviors create emotions that trigger the human brain to a "feel good" state. Like substance abuse, behavioral addiction provides a person with a burst of chemicals that keeps them stuck in an emotional dependence.

When a person cannot stop thinking about a given substance or behavior, it blocks their ability to handle emotions and seriously interferes with their daily tasks, work, relationships, and just about every aspect of their life. Common addictions are to drugs, alcohol, food, gambling, sex, love, shopping, exercising, working, video gaming, and social media. Some are more dangerous than others, but nearly everything that feels good can become addictive. Know anyone who is perpetually angry? Someone who feels the need to post every good deed on social media to fulfill their craving of "likes"? Missing out on time with family and friends because a video game is more appealing than reality? All addictions have one thing in common: they sap people of their power, disrupt and distort their energy, and subjugate their will.

We both have dealt with the devastating effects up close. Sandra's father was an alcoholic, and we both have lost friends and family members to the disease of dependency—notably our dear friend Salem Warlock Shawn Poirier, whose death we mourn to this day. Witches are not immune. Empaths and psychics can find themselves in the throes of addictions, even as they are helping counsel others who suffer from addictive behaviors. When these cycles trap us in negative patterns, we can turn to candle magic to break free.

Candle spells attack addiction in two major ways: (1) by using fire to separate a person from the habit or vice, and (2) by recalibrating and refocusing the person's energy away from the addiction and back on a healthy track. We have used candle magic to bolster motivation, boost strength, increase willpower, and short-circuit temptation. (Of course, we recommend that you seek the advice of medical or professional guides along the way.) These spells provide the user with the strength and conviction to make lasting positive changes in order to transform their life. They are extremely personal for us, and we share them with you along with our most sincere hopes for success should you ever need them.

BREAK THE CHAINS OF ADDICTION CANDLE SPELL

Please note: Many people do not have the willpower to overcome physical or mental dependencies by themselves. Candle magic is meant to be a magical support for professional help, not a substitution for it. Please reach out to a doctor and then use the following ritual to help tame any urges to continue unhealthy behavior patterns.

You need:
> Black chime or taper candle
> Heat-safe holder
> Letter opener or other pointed implement for carving
> Banishing or frankincense oil (see the Resources section of
> the Appendix)

Perform this spell on a Saturday for additional banishing force. Engrave the candle with the word or words that describe the addiction. Anoint the candle with banishing oil while chanting at least 10 times:

"All that takes my power, be gone,
 All that saps my will, be gone."

Place the candle in the holder and light it, then say:

"Candle of power,
 Candle of might:
 Banish addiction,
 Bring healing light."

Take any leftover wax to a place where two roads meet and bury it there.

BANISH BAD HABITS CANDLE RITE

Every October since 2002, Sandra has been leading a transformative ritual called Death and Rebirth as part of Salem's annual Festival of the Dead. This rite has been created in the spirit of that event. Rosemary and sandalwood together have a subtle but effective banishing energy that clears negativity but also helps lay the groundwork for good habits.

You need:
 White votive candle
 Heat-safe holder
 Rosemary oil
 Stick of sandalwood incense
 3×3-inch piece of paper

Larger paper (parchment if possible)
Black ink pen
Colorful pens or markers
Fire-safe dish or iron cauldron

Light the sandalwood incense and take three deep, cleansing breaths.

On the small piece of paper, write a word or phrase in black ink that sums up the habit you wish to leave behind. Do not put a lot of time or energy into this because you are getting rid of it.

On the larger piece of paper, describe the life you want for yourself. Include specific details. Make this as colorful as you wish. You can choose to draw a pentacle and place positive words in each point and the center, or just write out what you wish to manifest.

Anoint the white votive candle with the rosemary oil, saying:

"*I anoint and consecrate this candle*
That it may serve as a beacon here
And in the spirit world.
This wax represents my old way of being
That will be burned away."

Tuck the larger paper with your manifestation on it under the heat-safe holder. Place the votive candle into the holder, and light it, speaking your intention to the Universe:

"*This is the fire of my will,*
The passion of my new life consuming the old.

As this candle burns, my strength grows.
I will tend the flame of my new life,
Manifesting all good and leaving the bad behind,
So shall it be."

Holding one corner of the small paper with your bad habit on it, dip the opposite corner into the flame until it catches fire, and drop it into the fire-safe dish or cauldron to burn. Allow the white candle to burn all the way down. Bury any remaining wax with the ashes. Roll up the paper you wrote your manifestations on, and tuck it safely into your pillowcase, slip it under your mattress, or keep it on your altar if you have one.

BURNING A PETITION

WHERE THERE'S SMOKE, THERE'S FIRE

Cigarette smoking harms nearly every organ and can cause cancer almost anywhere in your body. It is also an expensive habit that takes everything from the smoker and gives back nothing. On the day before New Year's Eve 2012, Leanne smoked her last cigarette. She had hit her "enough is enough" point after a dynamic ritual on Halloween on Salem Common. While dancing around and raising energy with the crowd, she became faint. She realized that her labored breathing was affecting her connection to the Universe.

Leanne went home that night with bronchitis—and an overwhelming desire to quit smoking. She had tried to quit several times before, but this time was different. Leanne obtained the necessary weapons to defeat the hold tobacco had on her lungs and her psyche, arming herself with gum, hard candies, water, candles, a tumbled amethyst, and her freshly boosted willpower. It was New Year's Eve, and it was high time to transform her health.

The "Wonder Twin power" of candles and crystals cannot be overstated. Leanne burned many candles during those first few days, weeks, and months of being a nonsmoker. The dancing flame was a wonderful distraction from the pains and cravings she felt in the process of letting go of the habit, but she couldn't exactly take a candle everywhere she went. She passed an amethyst over the flame of the candle and always kept it with her to support her willpower during challenging times. She would meditate with the candle to help quell her anxiety during withdrawals; daily focus and meditation with the candle while holding the stone were a huge benefit.

Smoking, like many other addictions, is often a social behavior. Some of the most challenging times in the battle against dependency arise when other addicts are downplaying the situation and not taking your struggle seriously. Charging crystals with a candle before you spend time with other smokers helps with the direct and indirect pressure by releasing negativity and supporting your confident outlook. When a social situation arises and you feel challenged, hold the stones in your hand, remember the candle burning, and reaffirm your commitment to yourself. Sometimes just the grounding act of keeping stones tucked in your pocket (or your bra!) can be enough to refocus your will and recharge your motivation to stay the course.

QUIT SMOKING CANDLE MEDITATION

We are both former smokers, and we remember what it was like to quit. There are many options you can discuss with your doctor; no matter what path you choose, you can add candle magic to your arsenal.

You need:
    Black chime, taper, or votive candle
    Heat-safe holder
    Pen
    3×3-inch piece of paper
    Any combination of these 3 tumbled stones: amethyst,
        citrine, and peridot
    Black charm bag

On the paper, write the manifestation, "I am a nonsmoker." Arrange your tumbled stones in a triangle, place the paper in the center, and set the candleholder on top.

Light the wick and focus on the base of the flame. Take three deep, mindful breaths, inhaling through your nose and exhaling through your mouth with pursed lips, the way you might blow smoke. Imagine the toxins of cigarette smoke leaving your body in a noxious, filthy cloud with each expulsion of air. Keep in mind that the lungs are one of the fastest-healing organs in the human body. The moment you snuff out that last cigarette in the ashtray, your lungs are already fast at work repairing the damage.

Close your eyes. Visualize or think of yourself sitting near the edge of the ocean, hearing the crashing of the waves. Feel the sand cradling your body and the mist from the waves showering your face. Smell the clean ocean air, free from any tobacco odor, which will help clear your lungs. Open your eyes, carefully pass each stone through the fire, and place them in the black charm bag.

Let the candle burn in its entirety. Pick up the paper that was under it and read it out loud, with conviction: "I am a nonsmoker." Let your soul hear it, and more importantly, believe it. Remember and reflect on the reality that you weren't born a smoker. There was a time when smoking didn't dominate your life. Put the paper in the black charm bag along with any remaining wax, and carry it with you during the day to reinforce the fortitude of the spell.

POWER TRIO FOR
QUITTING SMOKING OR OTHER SUBSTANCES

Amethyst: Purification of body and mind. Amethyst is often used to aid in overcoming alcohol addiction. Ancient emperors who wanted to control their drinking would fill their cups with amethyst and wine to prevent intoxication.

Peridot: Reclaim your personal power and facilitate transformative healing. Peridot is popular in jewelry, so it can be easily worn or carried. It is second in hardness only to diamonds, so call upon it to strengthen your resolve to quit.

Citrine: Relieve peer pressure, release negativity, and build a confident outlook. Hold citrine in your nondominant hand and reaffirm your commitment to yourself.

WHEN NOURISHMENT BECOMES ADDICTION

Weight-loss and body-transformation stories have dominated the headlines of popular media for decades. What we're talking about in this section is more than society's idea of beauty and the general public's obsession with what celebrities look like. We are not advocating for anyone to change anything about themselves they don't want to change.

We have both been on a journey of health (Sandra since April 2019 and Leanne since May 2020), and it's not just about what size clothes we fit into, although losing weight has been a key part of restoring our energy, mobility, flexibility, and self-confidence. We have chosen to change our relationship with food in favor of having a healthy way of nourishing our bodies that reveal our best selves. We believe that we can love ourselves exactly as we are right now, while also working toward greater health and a longer, happier life.

We discovered that we had in common the need to seek something other than nourishment from food. It carried an emotional charge. Food was there when we were sad, anxious, hurt, worn out, or bored . . . and it was also there when we were celebrating, patting ourselves on the back, blowing off steam, or just hanging out with our loved ones. Food was comfort, companionship, even closure. But we were never really satisfied, especially with ourselves, and something had to change. We put in the work in the magical and mundane sense, and we got good results. But the work never ends. Our commitment is renewed each day. If this sounds familiar and you find that you are struggling to break a food addiction, this spell can help support your efforts.

FEED YOUR BODY, NOT YOUR ADDICTION: HEALTHY NOURISHMENT CANDLE SPELL

You are the caretaker of your physical body, and it is your ticket to experiencing all this life has to offer. Fuel your body with what it needs to take you everywhere you wish to go.

You need:
   White chime, taper, or votive candle
   Heat-safe holder
   Letter opener or other pointed implement for carving
   Cinnamon oil
   Iolite tumbled stone
   ¼ cup sea salt

On a full moon, carve your initials into the candle along with the symbol for the planet Venus and the symbol for Libra, which signifies balance. Anoint the candle with the cinnamon oil, place it in the holder, and light it. Run a bath, filling the tub at least halfway. Pour in the sea salt, and place the iolite in the bathwater. (If a bathtub is unavailable, place the sea salt and iolite on the floor of the shower.) Step into the water, and while you're in contact with it, visualize your body healthy and strong. As you wash your skin, imagine your unhealthy cravings washing off and running down the drain, and repeat this mantra: "I am full and complete, exactly as I am."

When you step out, dry off and then snuff out the candle until your next bath/shower, repeating the mantra each time. Carry the iolite with you at all times to reduce your cravings. It also can serve as a reminder to eat something that will nourish you when you are hungry but that food is not the answer if you only are seeking something emotionally.

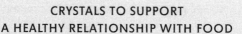

**CRYSTALS TO SUPPORT
A HEALTHY RELATIONSHIP WITH FOOD**

Iolite: Purifies and detoxifies the body on all levels.

Gaspeite: Cleans the clutter in your body, house, and mind. Helps you dispose of waste.

Howlite: Helps stop emotional overeating.

Shungite: Reduces inflammation and stress. Protects the body from electromagnetic frequencies.

LIFE SHOULDN'T BE WASTED:
ALCOHOL ADDICTION

People indulge in alcohol as a part of navigating social settings—and at times, as a form of escapism. Anyone can become prisoner to alcohol addiction; there are no prerequisites for that unwanted membership. It can quickly devolve to the point that every aspect of life has been turned upside down or even shattered beyond repair. Alcoholism causes myriad health, relationship/family, and workplace problems, all of which can lead to the king of them all: legal problems.

The fact that you're reading this chapter shows that you or someone you love may be experiencing some of the above-mentioned situations. If you feel that you are in the confining grips of alcoholism and you just can't get the upper hand in this battle for sobriety, it is time to give candle magic a chance. We have seen it reinforce recovery attempts and assist in supporting alcoholics to continue to make healthy choices and keep addiction at bay. This spell could trigger the lasting change that will turn it all around.

HALT THE DEMON ALCOHOL IN ITS TRACKS CANDLE SPELL

Alcoholics Anonymous talks about HALT: hungry, angry, lonely, and tired. These are conditions that can push a recovering addict toward temptation. Recognizing them can help minimize their effect. If you want to start turning the tide in this battle with the bottle (and that's just what it is, a lifelong battle), shining a light on the reason behind the desire to drink the moment the feeling hits and neutralizing it can be one of your secret weapons. This spell is another.

You need:
    Black chime candle
    Heat-safe holder
    Letter opener or other pointed implement for carving
    Peppermint oil (or chamomile oil)
    Amethyst stone
    Photo of alcohol of choice (rum, vodka, wine, and so on)
    Fire-pit, iron cauldron, or fire-safe dish

Place the photo of the alcohol in the center of a table. Carve the word *Alcohol* into the candle. Anoint the candle with peppermint or chamomile oil, place it into the holder, and light the wick. Hold the amethyst in your hand while you watch the candle burn to charge it with the energy of the disappearing word, indicating the influence of alcohol receding. Watch the word, *Alcohol,* melt before your eyes. Allow the calm feeling of control to wash over your body, mind, and spirit. After the last letter of the inscription has burned away, carefully ignite one corner of the photo with the remaining candle's flame and then place it in the fire-safe container. Let the candle burn itself out with your supervision. Afterward, carry the amethyst stone with you to keep the spell active.

WHEN THE MEDICINE BECOMES THE DISEASE: DRUG ADDICTION

As of this writing, the world is still fighting a decades-long opioid epidemic, and the epicenter is the United States. Prescription drug misuse and abuse has taken countless lives, and there seems to be no end in sight. Both of us have lost people in this war—and the ultimate battlefield lies within.

BREAK FREE OF DRUG ADDICTION 7-DAY CANDLE SPELL

We would never claim that candle magic alone can solve the problem, but it is a way to shore up strength for the fight. A candle-burning practice, combined with therapy and medical advice, can help the mind focus on healing rather than the pain and struggle of withdrawal. This spell serves to reaffirm a person's commitment to staying clean of narcotics and can be repeated as often as necessary.

You need:

> 3 7-day candles or tall pillars in glass hurricanes: 1 white, 1 red, and 1 black
>
> Empty pill bottle, copy of prescription, or other piece of drug paraphernalia
>
> 1 ounce nettle leaf herb
>
> ½ cup to 1 cup sea salt
>
> 1 square foot black fabric
>
> 1 yard red thread or ribbon

Place the representation of the addiction (bottle, prescription, or other) in the center of the black fabric square. Cover it in sea salt, pour the nettle leaf herb on top, and fold the fabric over it. Secure the fabric with the red thread or ribbon, wrapping it in a crisscross pattern until it is completely tied up. Knot it five times, and place it on a table or altar. Set the three candles around it in the shape of a triangle. Light the black candle and say:

"By the power of my will, this suffering will end."

Light the red candle and say:

"By the life in my blood, this battle will be won."

Light the white candle and say:

"By the light in my spirit, the darkness will be banished."

Allow the candles to burn for at least 1 hour. Snuff them out, and relight them each night for 7 nights, allowing them to burn for at least 1 hour each time. Whenever they are lit, speak the words above.

NOT ALL FUN AND GAMES: WHEN GAMBLING GOES TOO FAR

Gambling can seem harmless . . . until it's time to pay the bills. It is particularly devastating when it is discovered, too late, that people who have a financial responsibility to family have lost their bill money or life savings on the hopes of winning big. Gambling can also lead to other addictive behaviors, and even crime, as the addict seeks more sources of collateral to use in an attempt to win back their money, which is often a lost cause.

Few people understand gambling as a "real addiction" until they see firsthand the damage it causes. In truth, compulsive gambling is the most common impulse-control disorder, and it can lead a person, regardless of how successful they are, to complete and total ruin in a shockingly short amount of time.

AN APPEAL TO THE PATRON SAINT OF GAMBLING ADDICTION

St. Bernardine, "the Apostle of Italy," believed that addictive substances distracted people from God's blessings and is known for persuading the residents of Bologna to quit gambling. After hearing him preach, the residents burned all their cards and gambling tools. St. Bernardine is the Catholic patron saint of giving up gambling, and he has come through for people in Leanne's extended family when called upon.

You need:
> White 7-day candle
> Heat-safe holder
> Picture of St. Bernardine

Begin this candle magic on a Saturday. Place the picture of St. Bernardine in the center of the table. Position the candle next to the photo of the saint, and light it. While the candle is burning, say:

> *"St. Bernardine, give me the strength and the courage not to waste my money on games of chance."*

Burn the candle for 1 hour every day for 9 straight days.

MIGHT AS WELL FACE IT,
YOU'RE ADDICTED TO LOVE

True love is grand. New love is exciting. Obsession is dangerous.

Feeling a connection with an attractive person can be all-consuming—and it can be devastating when the feelings aren't mutual. Many refuse to let go of the notion that some cosmic relationship exists. We have counseled a staggering number of clients who have tried to force a romantic attachment, repeatedly calling, sending relentless texts, and stalking the object of their desire on social media.

The hardest aspect of working as a psychic is breaking a person's heart by saying the dreaded words, "They are just not into you." When Leanne informed one new client that the guy she was interested in was not her soul mate, she got agitated and asked for a refund. Over the next three months, this woman proceeded to get readings from everyone in downtown Salem, going from psychic to psychic to keep her fantasy alive. She spent hundreds of dollars on readings and spell components to try to change the outcome. She desperately wanted him to desire her the way she desired him. Finally, after almost a year, she came back to Leanne with the same question and asked for another love spell. She claimed she could "feel" him getting closer, even though they hadn't had contact in six months. That's when Leanne finally got through to her. She instructed her that it was time to cleanse the obsession from her spirit. With a new resolve, the woman left the shop with a banishing candle.

Sometimes, this obsessive behavior occurs after a breakup, when one partner can't move on. Whatever the case, spellwork can help. This is a multistep process.

STOP CARRYING A TORCH: LIGHT A CANDLE

Part 1: Operation Clean Sweep

You need:
> White tealight candle
> Heat-safe holder
> Myrrh incense stick
> White vinegar
> Cleaning cloth

"As within, so without." The best way to cleanse your mind is to clean your space, clearing it of any residual items or energies related to the obsession—but saving one photo for Part 2. Light the myrrh incense and allow the smoke to waft through the space, or carry it around counterclockwise for a more active cleansing. Wash any re-lated clothing and linens with white vinegar, and use the cloth to wipe down counters and other surfaces.

Delete and block all forms of contact.

Light the white candle, set it in a holder on a table, and sit quietly in front of it. Take several deep, cleansing breaths. Allow the light of the candle to cast off the heartbreak. Let the candle burn down all the way.

Part 2: Wash That Crush Right Out of Your Hair

When the space has been cleaned of all remnants of the object of obsession, it is time to purify your body.

You need:
Black tealight or votive candle
Heat-safe dish
½ cup kosher salt
Shampoo
The last remaining photo of the obsession

Pour the salt into the heat-safe dish. Place the black candle in the salt, and light the wick. Use the flame to carefully burn the photo of the person being obsessed over, lighting one corner of the photo and dropping it into the salt. As it is burning, say:

"May my eyes be freed from your sight,
I banish you from my heart and my life.
No longer will I toss and turn;
You are none of my concern."

Burn the photo until it is ash. Wash your head and hair with the shampoo, freeing your thoughts of the person being obsessed over. Allow the candle to burn in its entirety and then bury the ash and salt.

CHAPTER 8

IN MEMORIAM:
Mediumship and Vigil Candles

All around the world, people light candles to honor those who have crossed over into spirit. The candles serve as a tribute to those who have passed and a comfort to those who grieve. (The word *funeral* even has its root in the Latin *funus*, which means "torch.")

The ceremony of lighting a candle to honor a loved one can be traced back to pagan rituals, but candles figure strongly in the practices of every major religion. In the Christian faith, candles are traditionally white, symbolizing purity and representing the soul of the person who has died, and votives are often lit in churches or at gravesites. In Buddhism, candles represent the "light of Buddha's teachings" and are lit every day on an altar with offerings to meditate on the life of someone who has passed. In Judaism, a yahrzeit candle is burned for 24 hours on the anniversary of the death of a loved one, ensuring that they are remembered and their memory is treasured. Catholics mark All Souls Day by lighting candles to remember the departed and to carry prayers for them and for those of us still here. Candlelight represents life—a life lived and loved. Love is what makes it so powerful. No matter what faith path you have chosen, there is one constant: love never dies.

Lighting a candle reminds us that the spirit lives on. The flame burns away grief, and the light defeats the darkness of death. Even the simplest ritual promotes reflection and brings brilliance to our memories. Vigil candles are a lovely way to not only honor the life but also invoke the spirit of a loved one, or even an idol, who has passed into spirit. Many find using a memorial candle on special dates to be a comfort. It enables the grieving to connect with those who have died, which eases the pain of loss. Burning a memorial candle also feeds the spirit, so a connection can be built between the living and the dead.

On the anniversary of our friend Shawn Poirier's death, we celebrate his life by sharing a meal and burning a memorial candle featuring Shawn's photo to give him a place at the table. The candle helps us connect to his spirit, and we talk to him as if he has never left this earth, creating a bridge between this world and the next. Shawn was a talented psychic, and he continues to send messages from beyond the grave. You can visit our memorial altar for Shawn at Hex: Old World Witchery in Salem; we burn a candle for him there every day.

MEMORIAL CANDLES

Memorial candles come in many different styles. You can personalize yours using photos, quotes, names, and dates. The flicker of the flame behind the image of a friend or family member is a beautiful tribute (and sympathy gift), but it is also an effective way to communicate with those we have lost—because we never truly lose them. Our loved ones are still with us in spirit, and we can connect to them with a few uncomplicated rites. You can find memorial candles easily online or create your own with our candle-making instructions in Chapter 12.

Cultures all over the world create shrines or altars to the dead in their homes. You may have already done this, either purposefully or subconsciously. Do you have a shelf somewhere where you can place photos of your deceased loved ones with mementos and other treasures they gave you? You've got the makings of your altar already.

CANDLE SHRINE OF REMEMBRANCE

We love to see the shrines that our friends, family, and fans create, so please send us photos to share the tributes you create for your loved ones.

You need:

    White candle (any type, including battery-powered)

    Photos and/or mementos of the person or pet who died

Music that helps you remember the person who crossed over
Letter opener or other pointed implement for carving
Heat-safe holder
Glass of water or a favorite beverage

To create an atmosphere of remembrance, turn on some music your loved one relished in life. If you are using a 7-day candle, or a candle encased in glass, you could adhere a photo to the outside of the container. Otherwise, place your photo a safe distance from the candle along with the mementos. If you choose a votive, taper, or pillar candle, you may wish to carve the sides with significant initials, names, and dates. If you are using a tealight, you will probably only have room to carve initials and dates. If you can't safely have an open flame in your space, a battery-powered candle can help light the way home. Another advantage of flameless candles: they can be left to safely glow all night, maintaining the connection while you sleep.

Finally, leave a glass of water or a favorite beverage as an offering to their spirit. You may pour yourself a glass of the same and drink it to align with them. Water is a universal choice because water connects us all and is the element of intuition, so bringing water into the rite heightens your intuitive abilities.

This ritual can be done daily, weekly, monthly, annually, or to commemorate special days like birthdays and anniversaries.

A GLIMMER OF HOPE:
CANDLES AND MEDIUMSHIP

Death is life's greatest mystery. The heartbreak from the loss of a loved one can leave us empty, with questions, regrets, and concerns that many fear will never be answered. Grief can harm our minds, bodies, and spirits, so easing that anguish is vital to our health. For decades, our clients have sought assistance in their times of mourning, and we have done our best to bring some measure of comfort.

Over the past two decades, thanks to the attention television and the media have brought to the practice of mediumship, more people than ever have decided to consult a medium to communicate with their beloved dead. Mediumship is the gift of communicating with spirit. A medium is, literally, an intermediary between the spirit world and ours. Occasionally, mediumship can bring forth prophecies and visions of what will happen in the future, as those in spirit deliver messages of what is to come, but most of the time the messages are of a more personal nature.

Despite the images Hollywood may project, please know that to practitioners, mediumship is *not* a form of entertainment but rather a form of comfort and connection. That said, although the dead are not here for our amusement, they sometimes do amusing things. Shawn Poirier had a wicked sense of humor in life, and his trickster nature is still alive and well. He loves to introduce himself to new employees of the Salem shops Hex and Omen by repeatedly knocking things off the shelves at them and being a general nuisance until he gets attention. Most recently, he made his memorial poster board vanish for weeks and suddenly reappear in a different location in the back office at Omen. His most impressive trick is relighting his memorial candle on the shrine devoted to him at Hex after it has been snuffed out for the day, which he has done to more than one employee.

The awakening of our minds to mediumship manifests differently for us all. It is an ability we all possess, but most people never access it. We all have an inherent potential to make a connection to our beloved dead, but like all talents, it takes a willingness to try and dedication to practice. Trust and believe that your ancestors are waiting behind the light. They await the time you will notice the signs and signals they send to you in your daily life. The force of your love for them, and theirs for you, is astonishingly powerful. It is what we tap into when we act as your intermediary, but we can only dip into that well. You contain the entirety, and you can draw on all of it. As practiced as we are in the art of mediumship, your lack of practice is more than made up for in the remarkable tenacity of your attachment to those you love. Even death cannot sever it. So how do you begin to work with this bond?

Meditation is a vital component of mediumship. The conscious mind has to be relaxed in order to perceive the spirit world. Meditation silences the static and neutralizes any negative self-doubt. Be present in the moment, and trust that your loved ones are ready to speak with you.

CANDLE MEDITATION FOR SPIRIT COMMUNICATION

Choose a place in your home that is comfortable and a time when you will have a minimum of half an hour without any interruptions or obligations. Wear loose-fitting, nonrestrictive clothes.

Light your candle. This may be a memorial candle or a tealight. If you have created or purchased a spell candle for spirit communication, use that.

Sit comfortably and close your eyes. Breathe deeply, counting each exhale until you get to 10. When you are first beginning this practice, you may find a stray thought or two—or eight—invading this space. The idea is not to fret over it. Instead, acknowledge it and let it go.

After the tenth exhalation, open your eyes. Begin to unlock this gift by staring at the base of the candle flame. Take slow breaths, and bring a memory of the person you are seeking to contact into your mind's eye. If you are not able to visualize this, imagine the feeling of giving that person a hug or the sound of their voice. Speak their full name, followed by what you called them if you had a nickname or diminutive for them. Say, "I love you." Repeat their full name and nickname, and say, "I call to you." Repeat their full name and nickname, and say, "I welcome you." Continue to breathe slowly and deliberately, and open your mind and senses to any ideas, visions, or messages that come through. Messages can come in many forms; you may hear the laugh or smell the cologne of a loved one. It may take three to five minutes to feel a connection. If you're still waiting, repeat the words aloud and "listen" again with all of your senses.

If you wish to dream about your loved one, the best time to do this meditation is right before bed. Just be sure to snuff out the candle before falling asleep.

GROUP CANDLE MEDIUMSHIP: THE MAGIC OF SÉANCES

Candles are often lit during séances to attract spirits, and some mediums even communicate with the dead by watching the flickering of the flame, which is called candle scrying. A séance, which comes from the French word for "session" and the Old French word for "to sit," is a cooperative effort to summon those who have crossed over in order to communicate with them. A real séance isn't the theatrical exercise seen in horror movies. All you need is a group of open-minded people who have the intention of contacting the departed.

If you would like to host a séance, first consider who would be interested in attending. It's probably best to not invite the cynics, at least not for your first one. Skepticism won't discourage a determined loved one on the other side from making contact, but negativity, fear, and disbelief make for an inhospitable environment for attendees and spirits alike. All invited guests should bring items that link them with their loved ones and connect their loved ones to the living world. The more well-loved an item was, the greater the amount of stored energy it contains, and that energy becomes a beacon in the spirit world.

We find that having a playlist of music that reminds us of our lost loved ones helps create the desired atmosphere; you can also use meditation or relaxation music to set the tone. Either way, keep the music at a reasonable background volume, and if you are using your phone or computer to play it, be sure to enable the Do Not Disturb function.

Remind everyone present to turn off their cell phones—in fact, it's a good idea to turn off or even unplug all electronic devices in the room. And of course, the only light in the room should come from candles.

When beginning a séance, participants should be sitting comfortably, preferably in a circle around a table. The table may contain the personal artifacts of the departed, any other tools that can aid in communication (such as crystals, herbs, or incense, as noted in the following list), and of course, candles. We have used just about every kind of candle in our séances, but the most common choices are tapers (they make it easy to watch the flickering of the flame) or memorial candles encased in glass. White candles often represent spirit, and black candles absorb negative energy, so a combination of these works well. Light the candles and place whatever commemorative items your guests have brought with them.

Other items that can be placed on the table or in the room to help prepare the space include the following:

- Photographs of people, places, and things that trigger memories
- Incense or room spray in frankincense, lavender, clary sage, myrrh, jasmine, or mugwort
- Crystals such as lapis lazuli, moonstone, labradorite, amethyst, or clear quartz

One person should be designated to lead everyone in taking three deep breaths, in through the nose and out through the mouth. This is the moment for everyone to reflect on the people they want to reach. Encourage them to focus on the candles, which will act as a beacon for the dead. Each person can choose to remain silent or speak the name of the person they wish to hear from in turn. Now, take note of the candles. Are they flickering or still? If the candles flicker when a name is spoken, that may be a sign the person's spirit is present.

Each guest may wish to state a question out loud. The reaction of the flame is confirmation that spirit is coming through. (See Chapter 11 for more information on interpreting the language of the flame.)

TIPS FOR A SUCCESSFUL SÉANCE

Take extra care with preparations; they make all the difference.

Heighten your awareness through deep breathing and meditation.

Pay attention to all of your senses for signs.

Acknowledge any odd feelings.

Recognize the energy of people and places you may not have expected.

Record your experience to reflect on it later.

Express your gratitude to the spirits for their presence.

It is common to see things from the corner of your eye during a séance, and occasionally a spirit appears in the shadows of the room. Thoughts like daydreams may occur, so pay close attention to any ideas that pop into your mind because they may be messages for you or someone else at the table. Listen for high-pitched or extremely low tones, which can also be a method of communication. Leanne has heard music that ended up being relevant to visitors of her séances.

On one occasion, she started to sing a song that had special meaning for one attendee, validation that a connection had been made.

Along with candle scrying, there are a number of other ways to communicate with spirit during a séance.

The Power of the Pen: Automatic Writing

It's always good to record the messages received during your sessions, but automatic writing takes pen and paper to another level. Automatic writing, also called psychography, is the act of tapping into your psychic gifts to communicate written messages from those who have crossed over. When this is done during a séance, the atmosphere is already set, but you can do this on your own as well. In either case, begin by visualizing the spirit you are seeking and inviting them to guide your writing hand. If you have a specific question, you can write it out, or you can write the person's name over and over to call them and then let the words come as they will. Pay no attention to spelling, grammar, or the way the writing looks on the page; instead, **watch the candle flame while you write** rather than looking down at the paper. Imagine the spirit guiding your hand, and allow the pen to form words and phrases automatically. If thoughts come to you, write them down. Some messages don't make sense in the moment but become clear in the following days and weeks.

Leanne uses automatic writing in her séances and mediumship sessions. She fondly remembers a séance of 20 people practicing automatic writing in which half the participants wrote the name *Lena*. None of the guests could identify who Lena was, but Leanne knew— that was her own grandmother, waving hello from the other side.

COMMUNICATING WITH SPIRIT
THROUGH AUTOMATIC WRITING

Mood Swings: The Pendulum

Here's our favorite basic way to answer yes or no questions. Any object suspended at the end of a chain can function as a pendulum. For example, during a séance, the wedding ring of the deceased could be hung on a necklace. With your elbow on the table, hold the top of the chain and allow the ring to swing. Ask, "Show me yes," and watch the movement. Typically, it will swing forward and back, like someone nodding "yes." When it steadies itself back to a neutral position, ask, "Show me no," and watch the movement change. It will likely move from side to side, like shaking your head "no." (Spinning in a circle is considered the equivalent of "ask again later.") After you have established the direction for each of these responses, you can begin asking questions that require yes or no answers.

Moments of Reflection: Scrying Mirrors

When using scrying mirrors, you're peering at your own reflection in a black mirror to facilitate images from spirit. Chapter 11 offers an in-depth explanation of this powerful tool.

Hands–On Experience: Talking Boards

Talking boards, also called spirit boards or Ouija boards, are made of a flat sheet of paper or wood. The typical board contains images of the alphabet, numerals from 1 to 9 followed by 0, the words *Yes, No,* and *Good Bye.* Guests ask the talking board a question, and a movable pointer called a planchette highlights words or letters to spell out an answer.

Regardless of what you've seen in movies, talking boards are not evil. A talking board is a tool to speak to spirit and communicate with energy you may not understand. Despite the fact Parker Brothers manufactured the Ouija board as a game, it is to be taken seriously. Do not break it out while inebriated.

Start by lighting a white candle and setting an opening intention, such as "May the luminous light of this candle protect us, and guide the most correct spirits to us, for the good of all." When used in a group, one person should ask all the questions to avoid confusing the spirits. Everyone should place their fingertips on the planchette as the designated speaker asks, "Is a spirit here?" and "What is your name?" Be polite and respectful. Calm focus is imperative, especially when the pointer starts to move. Pay careful attention to the letters. Often, the way spirits communicate is not clear, and misspellings, abbreviations, and "code words" are common. Always have a pen and paper on hand to record messages because they may require some deciphering later.

When closing the session, say farewell. With everyone's fingertips on the planchette, move the pointer to the words *Good Bye*. Snuff out the candle, and thank the spirits for sharing their knowledge.

We are surrounded by the spirit world. A séance allows us to unite with it, and it can help us reunite with our loved ones—but they are not the only spirits we can communicate with through the magic of candles.

BEINGS OF LIGHT: SPIRIT GUIDES

A spirit guide connects a person with the Divine and the Divine within themselves. They are mentors that protect us, inform us, and feed our spiritual growth. These allies help direct mediums and psychics safely though the world of spirit. There are several different types of spirit guides. Some come along life's journey, while others are connections from past lives. Developing a relationship with a spirit guide can lead you on the path to an awakening of personal power and help you grow to your fullest and happiest potential.

Candles can help form a bridge between people and their spirit guides. Here are our recommendations for where to start.

Archangels: Archangels are the highest of echelon of heavenly spiritual power. To connect with them, and call upon their high angelic assistance:

Michael: Burn a red candle on a Sunday for holy protection.

Raphael: Burn a bright pale-yellow candle on a Wednesday for healing and psychic gifts.

Gabriel: Burn an orange candle on a Monday for ease of communication and inspiration.

Uriel: Burn a blue candle on a Thursday for wisdom when facing challenges, or for aid in helping others.

Guardian angels: Guardian angels are individual protectors of a person's body and soul. Burn a white candle on a Monday to connect with your personal guardian angel.

Animal spirits: This could be a pet who crossed over or the spirit of a creature that reminds you of a person's distinctive energy. Burn a brown candle on a Saturday, and watch for images and sightings of animals, either in dreams or in reality. (Sandra's first spirit animals were the dragon, wolf, and bat, and they have been with her since she was a child. Leanne has bonded with the spirit of the honeybee, which has a nurturing energy that keeps her grounded and strong.)

Ancestors: Your family stands by you, even beyond death. Those who knew and loved you are particularly loyal guides who can serve as a beacon of hope and growth as you travel through life. To call upon your ancestral spirits, burn a black candle on a Saturday.

Past-life connections: A soul who knew a person in a past existence is often still here out of pure devotion. Death cannot keep apart souls linked by love. Burn a purple candle on a Saturday to be gifted hidden knowledge of past lives or to call a linked soul back to you.

MEET YOUR SPIRIT GUIDE SIMPLE CANDLE SPELL

Welcome in a spirit guide the way you would greet a friend, because they have most likely been on your side and by your side for some time. This spell will help you connect with them.

You need:
>Purple votive candle
>Heat-safe bowl
>¼ cup water
>¼ teaspoon mugwort

Shortly before bed, pour the water into the bowl and then sprinkle the mugwort into the water. Place the votive candle in the water and light the wick. Looking at the base of the flame, say:

"Oh, guide of life, guide born of light,
>*Come and visit me this night."*

Allow the candle to burn for 1 hour and then snuff it out. Repeat for 3 consecutive nights.

Your dreams will begin to contain symbols and messages from your guides so be sure to write them down in a journal so you can review and analyze them later. Don't be discouraged if you do not get results right away. Wait a few nights and begin again. When practiced nightly, communications with spirit guides will begin to unfold.

CHAPTER 9

LET IT SHINE:
Brilliant House Blessing

Step away from the sage, and step into the light.

A lit candle contributes more than just illumination; its energy permeates a space and changes its vibration, making it warm and inviting. The cozy atmosphere and metaphysical oomph that candles produce can influence family, friends, and guests. Candles have been used in dwellings for as long as there have been wax and wick. Originally a household staple as a source of light, candles are more commonly used these days to help create a welcoming environment. But they are capable of much more than that.

A candle can turn any occasion into a celebration, a pizza dinner into a romantic interlude, and clear the stink out of a room. We are not just talking about whatever you cooked for dinner; we are referring to the icky energy that wafts off some people. A charged spell candle melts away a bad mood, incinerates negativity, and transforms sour grapes into fine wine.

NEW HOME/OLD HOME BLESSING RITUAL

Home is where your heart, head, body, and spirit live. It is the sanctuary of the soul. A dwelling is more than just an address; it is the comfort center of a person's life.

Moving into a new residence gives you a chance for a fresh start. When you turn the key in the lock and step across the threshold, you want to create your own environment, casting away the energy of past occupants' experiences there. Consecration of a home with the light of a candle banishes past energy and allows you to leave your own energetic mark. It also banishes a family's built-up stress, anger, and grief. Have a fight with your partner? This house blessing gets rid of the crummy feelings afterward. Recovering from an illness? Perform this spell to promote a healing environment. Suffering the loss of a family member? Ease your grief with this blessing.

You need:
> White pillar candle
> Black pillar candle
> 2 heat-safe holders
> Bowl of clean water
> ¼ cup salt
> Tray to carry items around the home

Before the ritual of blessing begins, be sure the home is clean. Wash the floors. Dust. Create a visibly clean and organized area. This helps prepare the space for the work.

Open all the doors and windows to banish any unwanted forces that will diminish the new energy in the home. Starting at the highest point in the home (such as an attic or top floor), light the black candle. Put three pinches of salt in the bowl of water. Walk around largest room counterclockwise, first sprinkling the salt and water mixture and then holding the black candle up at eye level and out in front of you as you walk. Push and direct the old energy pattern toward any open windows and any outer doors. When walking with the salt and water, declare with a strong voice:

"By the powers of Earth and Water,
I cast you out!"

Carrying the candle, state:

"By the powers of Fire and Air,
I cast you out!"

When clearing, cleansing, or banishing energy in a home, you should start at the top and work your way down because most places have their points of egress on the first and/or basement floors. By working from top to bottom, you can clear the energy and then close the main doors behind it. Think of it like sweeping a staircase: if you sweep the bottom step first, you then sweep every step above it onto the one below, making far more work for yourself to get the stairs clean.

Carry the salt and water and then the black candle around each room on that floor, repeating the words several times in every distinct space, and close each door and window after you have pushed out the energy. Move counterclockwise around that level, including any hallways, until that level is complete and then move down to the next floor and repeat until every room has been cleared.

When the entire house has been cleansed from top to bottom, you can begin to bless it from the bottom to the top. In the last room you cleansed, light the white candle. Walk around the room clockwise first with the salt and water and then with the white candle. Instead of banishing, summon blessings. When walking with the salt and water, proclaim:

"By the powers of Earth and Water,
I bless this home."

Carrying the candle, state:

"By the powers of Fire and Air,
I bless this home."

As you bless each room, you can state your specific positive intentions or prayers for that space. The blessing does not have to be denominational. Just think of it as a way to permeate your home with affection, harmony, well-being, contentment, and wealth. Repeat in each room on each floor until every room is blessed. Leave both candles burning where you can safely attend them, as a symbol of the new balance in the home.

CANDLE MAGIC, ROOM BY ROOM

We both have rooms that are dedicated to spiritual pursuits in our homes, but every room in the house can hold its own special magic. You will look at every corner of your domicile differently by the end of this chapter!

WITCHIN' IN THE KITCHEN

The kitchen is the heart of the home. It is also where magic originates. Since ancient times, people have gathered around the hearth to cook, eat, and share news both good and bad. Even to this day, most of us automatically gather in the kitchen, to celebrate, mourn, and everything in between. This is why kitchens have doubled in size in new homes recently, and people have taken down walls in older homes between the kitchen and the rest of the main floor common areas. No longer the lonely domain of the family cook and the occasional helper or two, this room has evolved into a place to welcome and entertain guests and even hold rituals. The first time Sandra and her husband stood in sacred space together, it was in her kitchen, with a group of local Witches in a circle around her black marble butcher block island that was set with all the necessary tools and complete with—you guessed it—candles. A lot of magic can be accomplished in the kitchen.

Whatever your day brings you, remember our motto:

Kettle on and candles lit.

HOME SWEET HOME

Who doesn't love walking into a home to the smell of something delicious? The scents of baked goods evoke feelings of comfort, and many of the ingredients used in pastries and cookies are also allies in spellwork.

Cinnamon awakens the mind and brings clear thoughts. It brings passion to lovers as well as prosperity to wallets. You can add a dash to the melted wax that collects in jar or 7-day candles to increase their potency because it is considered to fortify and accelerate spells.

Another dessert recipe staple not limited to culinary pursuits, vanilla has been valued for its benefits for hundreds of years—it was used by the Aztecs for medicine and healing. When a person lights a candle enhanced with vanilla oil, they get a heck of a lot more than a sweet smell in their hearth. Vanilla is calming, soothing, and brings good luck and love. Vanilla can trigger nostalgia and remind us of our lives in a simpler time.

KEEP THE PEACE CANDLE SPELL

Sandra and Leanne both stock up on scented candles. Guests to our homes will tell you we are never without an assortment of scents, with jars burning in multiple rooms, even our bathrooms.

As we have mentioned, white candles are our go-to ingredient to clear an area of negativity. White light is associated with protection and purification. Some believe it is the true color of the soul. White candles can also bring unity and harmony to the table. This spell helps settle difficult personal and family issues, which are often discussed over a meal, and restores the peace in the wake of heated debates.

You need:

>White jar candle
>Clear quartz crystal

>KEEP THE PEACE ANOINTING OIL:
>⅛ cup olive oil
>4 drops patchouli oil
>4 drops lavender oil
>1 drop mugwort oil
>1 drop hyssop oil

Mix the oil ingredients, dip the tip of your finger in the mixture, and coat the top of the white jar candle. While coating the wax (and avoiding the wick), imagine a glowing ball of white light in the center of your chest. Light the wick, and imagine the light in your chest and the light from the candle forming one large sphere of light around you. Visualize this light radiating outward, expanding to fill your home. Picture each room awash with pure white light. Pick up the clear quartz crystal, hold it in your dominant hand, and say:

> *"Light of love, brightly shine.*
> *All within these walls, be kind."*

Repeat the words three times. Place the crystal somewhere you can see it when you are spending time with your housemates. Store the oil in an airtight bottle.

Let the candle burn for as long as it can be attended. Relight it the next time you can safely monitor it. Continue to burn the candle each time you feel the need until it's gone. When it has extinguished itself, clean out the jar, and find a use for it in your kitchen.

Finish with a nice cup of chamomile tea to reduce anxieties and stimulate healing.

For continued blessings in the kitchen, make cheesecloth charm bags and fill them with herbs, lucky personal charms, and quartz crystal points. Hang them above the doorways for a happy home and abundance.

Herbs to banish the bad stuff: Sage, rosemary, and comfrey leaf
Herbs to inspire love: Basil, fennel, oregano, thyme, and lemon

CHEERFUL LEMON CANDLE MAGIC

Instantly feel energized and improve your vibe!

You need:
Yellow votive or tealight candle
White ceramic dish
Slice of lemon
Letter opener or other pointed implement for carving
A cheerful song!

Leanne always has a yellow candle burning in her kitchen. Her whole kitchen is yellow, in fact. On Sundays, she does this personal ritual for joyfulness: first, she opens her window curtains and rolls up the shades, letting in the sunshine. On a yellow votive candle she carves a bumblebee, which reminds her to stay busy, buzzing, and happy. Next, she places a slice of lemon in the center of a white ceramic dish to symbolize the blessings of the sun in all its glory. Then she places her candle on it. If you want to try something similar, you can layer the lemon to enhance the spell and use the entire lemon so none goes to waste. (Add a spritz of lemon to a bit of white vinegar to wipe down your counters, for example. The rest of the lemon can be used to flavor tea or shrimp for dinner.) Next, she raises energy by singing or even dancing around the kitchen (without a thought to the poor passers-by hearing her rendition of "Here Comes the Sun" through the open windows). Choose a song that lifts your spirits, and make a joyful noise in your own kitchen.

OUT, DAMN SPOT, OUT!

While scrubbing your kitchen of dirt and grime, clean your space of unwanted energy.

You need:
Broom or mop
Dustpan or mop bucket
Black candle (a large black pillar candle works best because
    it gives you plenty of room to work with)
Heat-safe holder
Letter opener or other pointed implement for carving
Sage oil

Think about the things you want gone from your life and the lives of those who reside with you, such as illness, anxiety, anger, disagreements, or debt. Carve words or symbols that represent these things into the candle. Doing this also creates furrows in the shaft of the candle for the oil to settle into. Dab some sage oil on your fingertips, and rub it into the candle. Place the candle in the holder, and light it.

Pick up your broom or mop, and clean your floor counterclockwise. As you sweep or mop, say:

"I sweep away problems,
  Far from this house,
  All that disturb us/me,
  Will be cast out."

When weather permits, Leanne does this with her doors and windows open. This kicks out any lingering BS around her family. After she is done sweeping or mopping, she tosses the dirt or dirty water out the front door, yelling, "Bye, Felisha!" or "Get out!" She occasionally gets looks from the neighbors, but it works.

After the cleaning ritual, you may choose to burn a green or pink candle to welcome in love, abundance, and camaraderie for all the members of the household.

MAGICALLY DELICIOUS: DINNER FOR TWO

For instant date-night vibes at home, there's nothing like a candlelit dinner.

You need:
   2 red taper candles (the tallest ones you can find for a truly
      elegant look!)
   2 heat-safe taper holders
   8 carnelian stones
   Rose oil
   Bonus: 2 red roses

Dinner will be more than delicious when shared with someone special while two tall red candles cast a romantic glow. The color red incites passion and lust and gets the blood pumping. When you set the table, place the two candles on the left and right about a foot apart so you will be viewing each other between the two lights. Arrange eight carnelian stones between the two candles in a heart shape, signifying unity and endless blessings. If you have red roses, place one in a vase to your left on the table, and scatter the petals of the other across the center of the table between the place settings. Dress the tapers in rose oil to add some fuel to the fire for a night to remember.

WHEN THE FOCUS ISN'T FOOD: KITCHEN AS OFFICE/STUDY/SCHOOLWORK STATION

In many homes, the kitchen doubles as the home office. It has become a center for remote working, online meetings, hybrid schooling, and entrepreneurial pursuits. Leanne and Sandra both remember studying at the kitchen table when they were in school. Adding a bit of candle magic helps with focus when you're working in the hub of the house.

You need:
> Blue tealight or votive candle
> Orange tealight or votive candle
> Heat-safe holders
> Tumbled fluorite
> Tumbled hematite
> Citrus room spray

Burning orange and blue candles helps minds of all ages absorb and retain knowledge. The color orange encourages enthusiasm and fascination, and blue invokes wisdom, and together they create a productive, fertile environment for learning and accomplishing mentally taxing tasks. Place the blue and orange candles next to tumbled stones of fluorite for focus and hematite for grounding. Be sure they are located safely away from any little hands while homework is being done. Lemon, orange, or generic citrus-scented room spray helps keep kids and adults alike alert and attentive, even during those long meetings that should have been an email.

BEDROOM

When Sandra was a teenager, she commissioned her first altar to be built short enough that she could slide it under her bed in her small, 10×11-foot bedroom. A woodworker in Salem who had a stall in Artist's Row built it to her specifications—she was the first Witch he had ever met. (He has since gone on to found the popular Trolley Depot.) Likewise, before Leanne was out of the "broom closet," her bedroom was where she kept her altars and statues of worship.

The bedroom is a place of both peace and passion, a sanctuary where magic can be manifested. This chamber is where secrets live, too. It is the domain of loving, emotional release, and praying. Like us, many spiritual people who have limited space set up a shrine or altar in their bedrooms, and candles play a number of roles here, lighting the way to everything from a successful night's sleep or a compelling dream experience to a satisfying night of lovemaking.

"TO SLEEP, PERCHANCE TO DREAM"

We are such stuff
As dreams are made on,
and our little life
Is rounded with a sleep.

—WILLIAM SHAKESPEARE,
THE TEMPEST, ACT 4, SCENE 1

The dream world has always been associated with magic. When the body rests, the spirit travels. We've all heard the irrefutable scientific evidence on the importance of sleep for your body, mind, and spirit, but millions of people still suffer from sleep loss.

Working with candles can create an energy of peace and calm in the bedroom. The element of Fire will burn away mental and emotional burdens and calm the restless spirit. Using essential oils on your candles can also help you get a better night's sleep and retain your dreams upon waking.

You need:

Purple votive or pillar candle

¼ teaspoon mugwort

¼ teaspoon gardenia

2 cups clean water

Heat-safe glass bowl

Tumbled moonstone

Tumbled amethyst

Journal or notebook and pen

SLEEP HELPERS

Colors: Purple, silver, dark blue, indigo, and white

Herbs: Catnip, celery seed, chamomile, frankincense, gardenia, lavender, mugwort, and valerian

Crystals: Amethyst, aquamarine, moonstone, opal, quartz, sandstone, selenite, and turquoise

Meditate before bed. Use an indigo candle to promote peace.

Keep your sleeping area clean and free of clutter.

Avoid foods with added sugar.

Listen to vibrational music.

Write out your problems in a diary. This banishes the day-to-day strife from the brain.

Avoid caffeine in the evening.

Practice more meditation! ☺

In a glass bowl big enough to hold 3 cups of water, pour in 2 cups. Next add the moonstone and amethyst. Moonstone channels lunar Goddess energy that helps protect you while you rest and magnifies your intuition. Amethyst is also a go-to psychic power stone and promotes an atmosphere of tranquility. Sprinkle in the mugwort and gardenia, and place the candle in the center of the bowl. Light the candle. Then, as if speaking to the candle, say:

"Mother Moon, Queen of Night,
Help me sleep deep tonight."

As the candle burns, write down all the day's emotions that you are still hanging onto: happiness, anxiety, stress, excitement, anger, frustration, disappointment, attraction, fear, or embarrassment. Whatever you experienced that is staying with you, get it all out. Tell yourself that you can let go of all these feelings now, that it is time to rest and you can pick things up again in the morning, when you will be stronger and better able to process them. You can repeat the words again just before you close your eyes and drift off.

PROPHETIC DREAMS

When the human consciousness rests, the soul and spirit rise. This allows for vivid dreams that can connect us with psychic information from the collective unconscious, the higher self, and the Divine, as well as messages from our ancestors, spirit guides, and lost loved ones.

Candles anointed in lavender oil relax the busy mind. Lavender is known to bring prophetic dreams, and the candle flame serves as a watchtower that shines like a beacon in the realms of spirit.

You need:
  Blue or purple chime candle
  Heat-safe holder
  Lavender oil
  Journal or notebook and pen

DREAM HELPERS

Colors: White, indigo, purple, and lavender

Herbs: Basil, bay leaf, copal, frankincense, gardenia, jasmine, lavender, mugwort, myrrh, nutmeg, patchouli, rosemary, sage, and wormwood

Keep a dream journal and make a habit of writing in it as soon as you wake up.

Meditate before bed, even just for a couple of minutes.

Rosemary is particularly prized for helping us remember our dreams. It also is known for helping facilitate a dream visit from someone who has crossed over. Put a dab of rosemary oil on your pillow at night, or make a simple sachet of rosemary and lavender using a square of fabric. Place 2 tablespoons each of rosemary and lavender in the center of the fabric, gather the edges, tie a ribbon around the bundle of herbs to secure it, and tuck the charm into your pillowcase before bed.

Before bed, anoint a blue or purple chime candle with lavender oil, and place it in the candle holder. Light the wick. Open your journal, and write these words at the top of a page:

"*Guardian spirits, while I sleep*
Guide my soul with wisdom deep."

At this moment, call upon any divine being or spirit comfortable for you. (Leanne calls upon the Great Mother of the Moon,

Artemis.) You can ask direct questions or state a simple request, such as, "Please show me what I need to know." After you have stated your intentions, place the journal under your pillow. Meditate for a few minutes on any questions or concerns you have raised. When you feel the time is right, extinguish the candle and go directly to bed. Don't look at your phone. Do not let anything disturb your peace. Upon waking, write down whatever you remember in your journal, starting beneath the words you wrote the night before.

SEXY TIME

Simply put, the bed isn't just for sleeping. We've helped countless couples light or reignite their fire. Let's just say the candles were only the beginning.

PASSION PLEASE CANDLE SPELL

Red penis candle or red vagina candle (Choose one or more
    to represent your desire. See the Resources in the
    Appendix.)
½ teaspoon damiana
¼ teaspoon cinnamon
2 drops ylang-ylang oil
Mortar and pestle
Heat-safe plate

Perform this spell on a Friday before the moon is full. Grind the damiana and cinnamon together with the mortar and pestle using clockwise motions. Anoint the candle(s) with the ylang-ylang oil, followed by the herbal blend. Begin to visualize the foreplay that would most turn you on. Take your time rubbing in the components, paying attention to every crevice. This will create the vitality for the spell.

After the candle is coated, light the flame, which represents the passion between the lovers. Spend at least 10 minutes focusing energy on the flame while thinking of your needs and desires. Watch the flame dance, visualizing the partners entwining as one. When you feel the climax of the energy, the spell is completed. Snuff out the flame and bury the candle's remains, giving the herbs back to the earth.

ADVICE FOR LOVERS

Colors: Red, and rich and dark shades of pink

Herbs: *Faithfulness:* Cayenne, chickweed, clover, elder, licorice, pepper, rhubarb, rosemary, and walnut

Fertility: Belladonna, hazel, oak, poppy, mistletoe, and mustard

Passion: Cumin, cinnamon, dill, garlic, orchid, mint, and saffron

Never end your night on an angry tone. Always kiss your love and wish them sweet dreams.

BATHROOM

We spend the first nine months of our existence surrounded by water. Perhaps this is why soaking in the bathtub is such a comforting experience. Doing candle magic while relaxing in a bath naturally increases your connection to the Divine. Wash away self-doubt and fear, and allow the water to carry your concerns down the drain. Water is a psychic energy conductor and amplifier, so your will and desire will echo throughout the Universe.

Removing the negativity that hinders a person from reaching their fullest potential and freeing their mind starts with cleansing, and both Fire and Water share this power. The flame of the candle helps burn away what we no longer need in our space, and by bathing in its light and heat, we are wrapped in the magic of our highest hopes and best intentions.

WASHING AWAY A BAD DAY CANDLE SPELL

We've all had them: the days where if it could go wrong, it did. Rather than let the events of the day govern your mood, shift the energy with this quick and easy spell.

You need:
Blue chime candle
2 drops chamomile oil
2 drops lavender oil
Heat-safe holder

Draw a warm bath. As the tub is filling, work the oils into the candle. Hold it between your palms before you light it, and chant the words "Peace and calm" until the mantra becomes a soothing hum to your ears. Place the candle safely in its holder, light the wick, and enter your bath. As long as you are not allergic, we recommend using 2 more drops each of lavender and chamomile oil in the bath, or, if you have access to it, hanging it fresh in the room. As you sink into the water, clear your mind. If any thoughts of the day's events come to you, allow them to fade and melt away. The light of the candle and the warmth of the bath dissolve them. When you feel calm and comforted, pull the plug and send any bad vibes down the drain.

SLIP INTO SOMETHING SEXY CANDLE SPELL

Red represents lust, passion, and a smorgasbord of earthly desires. This quick and easy spell will heat up a lot more than the candle wax.

You need:
    Red chime, tealight, votive, or pillar candle
    Ylang-ylang, sandalwood, or lust oil (see the Resources in
        the Appendix)
    Heat-safe holder

Preparing for a night of love and passion, anoint a red candle with your chosen oil, place it safely in the holder, and light it. Catch the blue part of the flame in your gaze and say:

"Let me feel the passion and the pleasure of the fire of life."

Slip into a warm bath or hot shower. As you wash your body, focus on your desired partner. Set your imagination free. After you towel off, stand naked in front of the candle. Dowse the flame and say:

"The fire has blessed me."

You can choose to slip into a sexy outfit—or maybe nothing at all.

YOU DON'T HAVE TO GO HOME, BUT YOU CAN'T STAY HERE: GETTING RID OF UNWANTED COMPANY CANDLE SPELL

Sharing space with cherished visitors is terrific . . . until they just will not go home. We all have people in our lives, however much we love them, who just don't know how to disengage from a good time. When cleaning up, yawning, and putting on your pajamas after showing them album after album of decades-old family vacation photos is not enough of a hint, a special "bye-bye" candle may be needed. It's good to keep a few of these on hand. Prepare them ahead of time, during the waning moon, and store them in a leakproof container for any occasion when company won't budge. (We can neither confirm nor deny putting some of these to good use to get noisy neighbors to move out.)

You need:
    Black chime candle
    Heat-safe holder

Leakproof storage container
Small mixing bowl
Rubber gloves

BYE-BYE OIL:
¼ teaspoon kosher salt
Pinch black pepper
¼ teaspoon mint leaves
¼ teaspoon hot sauce
Olive oil

Combine the oil ingredients in a small mixing bowl. Wearing the gloves (because of the spicy nature of this combination, don't skip the gloves), rub the mixture onto the black chime candle. Store the candle in the leakproof container until needed.

When guests are overstaying their welcome, light this candle in a holder and place it safely near a door or window. Take a moment to visualize the house calm and quiet again.

CHAPTER 10

THE FUTURE LOOKS BRIGHT:
Ignite Good Luck, and Burn Away the Bad

Luck can be defined as random energy that creates good and bad events in a person's life. Carl Jung described it as "a meaningful coincidence." The word originates from the Dutch *luc*, a shortening of *gheluc*, which means "happiness and good fortune" and dates back to the fifteenth century as a gambling term. We call beneficial, rewarding energy "good luck" and damaging energy "bad luck." If we agree that luck is just another form of energy, it can be harnessed, controlled, and mastered.

We've all had days when it feels like we've got a black cloud over our heads. Clients have sought us out at times when they felt figuratively or even literally cursed. Candle magic can lead to a change in mind-set and perspective and spark a much-needed shift in fortune. The element of Fire is associated with both purification and transformation, perfect for burning away the bad stuff and transmuting it to your advantage.

Here are some of our tried-and-true methods for clearing up the clouds, breaking a losing streak, and leading a charmed life.

MAY THE ODDS BE EVER IN YOUR FAVOR— GOOD LUCK CANDLE SPELL

It has often been said that life is just one big game of chance. If that's true, we could all use a nudge once in a while to make positive things happen. One of the ways we try to tip the odds for our clients as well as ourselves is by taking a psychic look into the future, whether via tea leaf or Tarot readings. For this good luck formula, we call on the archetypes of the Tarot, which are fueled by hundreds of years of usage and faith, and can unlock centuries of power.

This spell works best on a Sunday, but it can be started any time during a waxing moon phase.

You need:
3 yellow or gold taper or votive candles
3 heat-safe holders
Letter opener or other pointed implement for carving

3 Tarot cards: the Sun, the Ace of Pentacles, and the
    Wheel of Fortune
Bonus: success or solar/citrus oil

Carve the words *Good Luck* on the first yellow or gold candle.
Carve the word *Windfall* on the second candle. Finally, on the third,
engrave *Blessings*. If you have success oil, or a citrus or solar oil blend,
anoint each of the candles.

Lay the Tarot cards in a triangle, with the Wheel of Fortune at
the top, the Ace of Pentacles in the lower right, and the Sun in the
lower left. Place the Good Luck candle in its holder above the Wheel
in the top position, place the Windfall candle in its holder above the
Ace of Pentacles, and place the Blessings candle in its holder above
the Sun card.

Light the candles in the same order. As the candles burn, repeat
the following words three times:

"Wheel of Fortune, hand of fate,
 Turn my way with blessings great.
 Trio of the many graces,
 Make sure I hold all the aces.
 By the power of the Sun,
 I speak this spell, and see it done."

Place the Tarot cards where you can see them every day to reinforce the spell. For extra potency, leave the Sun card in a place that
exposes it to direct sunlight throughout the day.

WINDS OF CHANGE LUCK CANDLE SPELL

When life has been one mishap after another, stop the dominos from falling. Break out this black candle spell to take back control over your luck.

You need:
>Black chime, taper, or pillar candle
>Letter opener or other pointed implement for carving
>Heat-safe holder
>Kosher salt
>Olive oil
>4×4 inch sheet of paper
>Pen
>Cast-iron cauldron or cooking pot

In the black candle, carve an upward-pointing triangle with a horizontal line through it, which is the symbol for the element of Air. Anoint the candle with olive oil and then rub with kosher salt. Place it in the candleholder, light the candle, and say:

"The trouble of the past is gone,
It vanishes like night at dawn.
The winds of change are on my side,
Good luck with me will now abide."

Write down on the paper key words that sum up whatever has been causing you strife. Carefully dip the edge of the paper into the candle's flame until it catches fire and then drop it into the cauldron to burn. Scatter the ashes into the wind.

THE RAINBOW LEADS TO THE POT OF GOLD: LUCK OF EVERY COLOR

Different candle colors can be used to represent a variety of situations that need a little luck. Light the candle and say, "Lucky day, lucky day! Welcome, blessings! Come my way!" Any shape will work, but chime or tealight candles are best for these quick spells.

Red: Get lucky between the sheets or fight the evil eye

Orange: Bring fast luck in contracts, communications, companies, and court

Yellow: Grant luck and richness and help gamblers win in games of chance

Green: Generate opportunities to create wealth and financial growth

Blue: Bestow luck with interviews and tests and when dealing with authority figures

Indigo: Awaken the higher self to give you an advantage in decision-making

Violet: Ignite the imagination for creative problem-solving and help remove obstacles

White: Shine as a beacon of hope for improving luck in your life

Black: Burn away bad luck when fate hasn't been a friend

THE LUCKY BREAK—
CAREER OPPORTUNITIES KEY AND CANDLE SPELL

Stuck in the same dead-end job? Hoping for a promotion? Looking to change your career path entirely? This candle spell brings more opportunities for advancement and change.

You need:
>Yellow taper or pillar candle
>Heat-safe holder
>Letter opener or other pointed implement for carving
>Self-igniting charcoal disc (see the Resources section)
>Incense burner or heat-safe dish to hold charcoal
>¼ teaspoon cinnamon
>½ teaspoon peppermint
>1 teaspoon chamomile
>Mortar and pestle
>Almond oil
>Old skeleton key

Engrave the candle with your name, and draw a star over it and an old-fashioned skeleton key under it. (Do not worry about how well you can draw. Just do your best.) Combine the cinnamon, peppermint, and chamomile into the mortar, and grind into a powder with the pestle. Anoint the candle with almond oil, and rub with ¼ of the herbal mixture while visualizing the position or career desired. Then, light the charcoal and put the remaining herbal mixture on it. Pass the candle through the smoke nine times. Place the candle into the holder, and light the wick. Speak these words aloud:

"I call upon my lucky star
To show me where the best jobs are.
Light up the path that works for me,
Unlock the door with wisdom's key."

Pass the key through the smoke of the burning herbal mixture nine times, and rest it by the candle. Let the candle burn down completely. Bury any remaining wax in the earth. Carry the key while job hunting, interviewing, or discussing possible positions with your employer.

GAMBLING AND GAMES OF CHANCE

If we had a dollar for every self-styled comedian who asked us for the lottery numbers over the years, well, let's just say we'd be writing this book from an island in the Caribbean. Witches can't dole out the winning digits, but we do have our ways of coming out on top. We're happy to share the secrets we've learned because we know there's enough to go around, and around.

WINNER, WINNER, CHICKEN DINNER

Leanne learned this little bit of magic from a complete stranger while on a trip to Las Vegas. She had been playing a slot machine, and the house was winning again. More than a half hour invested and not one penny in the black. Her mojo was off, and she knew she needed something to change it. A woman appeared seemingly out of nowhere and sat down at the next machine. She looked fabulous, like some kind of Gambling Fairy, with her good luck charms around her neck, around her wrists, and attached to her "player's card." Muttering under her breath, she stroked the machine lovingly and placed a battery-powered tealight and a photo on top. She took out a crisp $20 bill and slid it into the machine. Leanne tried to look casual as she strained to hear what the woman was saying. She heard it again, something about chicken, then the Fairy called out, "Jimmy, don't fail me!" Leanne thought to herself, *Only in Vegas.*

Then, magic. The slot machine went off like a firetruck, with bells ringing and lights flashing. She had won $5,000. The Gambling Fairy was pleased. She picked up the photo and started talking to it, saying, "Thank you, thank you." Leanne looked at this peculiar woman and said, "Congratulations! I wish I had that kind of luck." The woman looked at her dead serious and said, "You got the luck. You just don't know how to use it. I get all my luck from my husband. He passed away." She patted the tealight resting on the slot machine and said, "This candle lights his way to me." Fascinated, Leanne inquired about what she had been saying to the machine. The woman proudly said, "Winner, winner, chicken dinner! Jimmy, help me win big!"

The following day, Leanne took some of the money she hadn't gambled away yet and bought a pack of battery-powered tealights before she headed to the casino. Apprehensively, Leanne stood in front of the slot machine. It was waiting for her like a handsome lover who always disappoints. She took a deep breath and put the candle on the machine. She didn't have a picture, so she closed her eyes and thought of her uncles, Sonny and Vinny, who loved gambling and Las Vegas. She then rubbed a $20 bill on the little plastic candle, slipped the money into the machine, and said out loud, "Winner, winner, chicken dinner! Uncle Sonny, Uncle Vinny, give me luck!" Leanne won $3,000 that day, the most she had ever won while gambling. She still wishes she could track down the Gambling Fairy to thank her for the tip.

FAST LUCK CANDLE SPELL

Bay leaf, also known as bay laurel, was historically fashioned into a crown or a garland to be worn by winners. It has been associated with the Greek god Apollo since ancient times, and over the years, it has been credited with keeping people safe from all manner of ills, including epidemics, devils, and ironically even Witches. It is also believed to aid in both the manifestation and protection of good fortune. Sandra keeps a jar of bay leaves she picked from a tree in the swamp of Louisiana on her healing altar, next to a statue of Apollo, and Leanne uses this spell right before a trip to the casino.

You need:
> Green taper or votive candle
> Heat-safe holder
> Letter opener or other pointed implement for carving
> Bay leaf
> Magic Marker
> Gold charm bag

Begin this spell on a Sunday. Write your name on one side of the bay leaf and the word *Win* or *Luck* on the other. Carve a dollar sign (or other currency symbol) and your name on the candle. Place the candle in the holder and light the wick. As the flame rises, meditate on winning, seeing yourself with a pile of money in front of you. Let the candle burn until it is extinguished. Fill the gold charm bag with any leftover wax and the bay leaf, and carry the energy of winning with you.

FRIENDS IN HIGH PLACES:
APPEALING TO THE DEITIES OF LUCK

Spirits, saints, angels, and Gods have been hearing our prayers and appeals for as long as there have been belief systems. It can be tempting to think of these entities as if they are genies granting wishes all day long, but that's not how it is. When forming a bond with a spirit ally or deity, you must feed the relationship to benefit from it. If you spend time communicating with and honoring higher powers, they may bestow their blessings. You're free to work with as many as you wish, but keep in mind that you need to devote time and energy to all of them, and no one has an endless supply of those.

Goddess of Luck: Fortuna

Leanne: *Fortuna is the Roman Goddess of fortune, chance, and fate. Much like the Greek goddess Tyche, She has been a symbol of blind luck and fate for centuries. I have a shrine to Fortuna in my bedroom, where I give Her crystals known for luck and good fortune. Weekly, I light a gold or green tealight candle in Her honor. Nightly, I place my spare change accrued over the day in an offering bowl at Her feet. When the money gets to be overwhelming, I donate it to animal rescues and other charities.*

You need:
> Statue or image of Fortuna or Tyche
> Gold candle of any size or shape
> Heat-safe holder
> Stick of frankincense

Create a shrine with a statue or image of Fortuna or Tyche. Burn the frankincense and light the candle. Take a moment to look at the flame. Close your eyes and meditate on all the blessings that have been offered to you throughout the day. Speak out loud simple words of gratitude and a petition for help with obtaining luck in your day-to-day life. It does not have to be complex or detailed.

STATUE OF THE GODDESS FORTUNA

If you wish to make a specific request, state it and write it on a piece of paper. Place the paper under the candle.

On Sundays, I take additional time and care when working with the Goddess. I speak out loud the following translation of a traditional hymn to Tyche (but it suffices just fine for Fortuna, too) while looking at the base of the candle's flame:

Orphic Hymn to Tyche, the Goddess of Fortune

"With prayer in mind, I summon you here, Tyche, noble ruler,
  Gentle Goddess of the roads, for wealth and possessions,
As Artemis who guides, renowned, sprung from the loins of
    Eubouleus.
Your wish is irresistible.
Funereal and delusive, you are the theme of men's songs.
In you lies the great variety of men's livelihood.
To some you grant a wealth of blessings and possessions,
While to others, against whom you harbor anger, you give evil
    poverty.
But, O Goddess, I beseech you to come in kindness to my life,
And with abundance grant me happiness and riches."

God of Good Fortune: Ganesha

Sandra: *If you know me, you know my patron is Ganesha. He chose me way back when I was in the fourth grade—but I didn't recognize Him until I was in college. I remember standing in my grade-school gym during the bazaar, holding a glass elephant in my hand. It had one broken tusk, but in my eyes, it was beautiful. I asked the adult manning the table how much she wanted for it. She remarked with disdain, "Oh, it's broken." I said, "I know, but I still want it." She turned to the adult at the next table and laughed, "She still wants it!" Her words stung me. I couldn't understand why she would make fun of me for accepting the little work of art exactly as it was. I lost a bit of my innocence in that exchange and walked away with my treasure feeling angry but determined not to let her narrow view change mine. A decade later, I would come to work for my first teacher in the Craft, Richard Ravish, who would introduce me to the beautiful and humble elephant-headed God—with the broken tusk.*

The Hindu god Ganesha has the head of an elephant and a human body. He is said to have three wives, and each of them symbolize a differ-

GANESHA GHEE CANDLE BURNER

ent blessing: intelligence, prosperity, and success. He is the God of good luck and beginnings, and He is honored first at the start of any worship.

Ganesha is often called the Remover of Obstacles; this is one aspect of His power. He is actually the Lord of Obstacles, as there are times when He has to place boundaries and limitations for good reasons.

One traditional way to honor Ganesha is to light a ghee candle. There are some beautiful candleholders that are specifically designed for this.

You need:
  1 cup ghee (clarified butter)
  Cotton wicks, as many as you want to prepare (see the
    Resources section)
  Saucepan
  Airtight container

Heat the ghee to liquefy it. You can place it in a saucepan over low heat, or you could place it in a heat-safe container and set that into a pan of hot water.

Pick up a cotton wick, if it has thin and thick ends, hold the thin end and submerge the rest of the wick in the liquefied ghee for a minute. Take it out for a moment to dry slightly, and repeat twice more. Allow the wicks to cool and harden, and store them in the airtight container. When you are ready, place one in a fire-safe container and light the wick.

Many mantras can be spoken as part of the rite, if you are so inclined. This is an English translation of one of the most important of them, the Siddhi Vinayak Mantra:

"O Lord of Wisdom and Happiness, only you make every endeavor and everything possible; you are the remover of all obstacles and you have enchanted every being in the Universe, you are the Lord of all women and all men."

As always, speak from the heart. He will appreciate that. Ganesha also loves sweets, so leave Him fruits or candies.

GOOD AND BAD LUCK, ITALIAN STYLE: LEANNE'S FAMILY TRADITIONS

Our beloved ancestors are bridges that connect us to the Universe and the spirit world. Their wisdom and traditions protect us and teach us valuable lessons. Leanne grew up in an Italian American family. Italian magic is folk magic. Just like a "Sunday gravy," every family and every region has its own particular way of using candles for luck and controlling chance. These are some common and not-so-common practices of Italians in America and are personal to Leanne's private practice.

GET LUCKY

The number 13 is lucky in Italy, especially when gambling. (Although many Italians believe sitting down to a table with 12 others is bad luck.) It is also associated with the Goddess Fortuna and the lunar cycles, and known to bring prosperity and abundance in life. In Italy, charms for luck are made on Friday the 13th. Burn 13 gold or yellow tealight candles on Friday the 13th to ensure a lucky year.

ST. CAYETANO LUCKY CANDLE SPELL

St. Cayetano, or Cajetan, is the patron saint of gamblers, good fortune, and the unemployed, and he can help you win big. Italian lore says the people would ask him for a favor and bet him a rosary he couldn't come through. Because he always did, he was able to get people to pray more.

You need:
Image of St. Cayetano
Green 7-day candle
Rosary beads

Begin the spell on a Sunday, during the waxing moon. Place the candle in the middle of the strand of rosary beads. Light the candle, saying:

"Saint of luck, son of light,
Grant me luck this day and night."

Burn the candle for an hour each day, repeating the words every time the candle is ignited, until it extinguishes itself. Take the rosary beads with you when gambling.

MALOCCHIO: THE EVIL EYE

The *malocchio*, also called the "evil eye," is one of the most ancient superstitions in Italy and throughout much of the Mediterranean. Every region seems to possess its own version, but all bring bad luck to the victim by carrying negative energy often caused by jealousy and envy. But not every hex is caused on purpose. Even good, well-meaning people can and do experience feelings of inadequacy, which can infect everyone in their world with trouble and strife. This is the root of the evil eye.

Italians perform a magical rite to see if a person has been afflicted with the evil eye. Traditionally, the breaking of the evil eye ritual should be taught on Christmas Eve by lighting a black candle to reveal hidden knowledge and then dropping olive oil in a plate of water. If the oil forms one large drop in the shape of an eye, it's a sure sign of the *malocchio*. Then scissors, a needle, and/or a silver steak knife is stabbed into the pool of oil, thus breaking the curse of the evil eye. Light a white candle to banish any residual negativity, and light both black and white candles to eliminate all bad luck and evil. While the candles are burning, say, "*Occhi e contro e perticelli agli occhi, crepa la invida e schiattono gli occhi,*" which means, "Eyes against eyes and the holes of the eyes, envy cracks and eyes burst."

Eggs and red candles are another method of removing the evil eye. The practitioner prays over the egg, saying the Hail Mary three times, and passes the egg over the flame of a red candle. The egg absorbs the evil and then it is broken and tossed into the toilet to be flushed away.

ITALIAN LUCKY CHARMS

These charms banish bad luck and protect the wearer or the place it is adorned. Bless these items by passing them over a flame.

Corno, or Cornicello

The *corno* ("horn") is a twisted, horn-shaped Italian amulet of ancient origin, primarily found in Italy and in America among descendants of Italian immigrants, that is hung or worn for protection against misfortune and the evil eye. You may have seen one dangling from someone's rearview mirror; hanging over a door, it brings financial rewards and protection from strife. These little horns, like those of all horned animals, are presumed to have once been sacred to the Old European moon Goddess, Diana, before the rise of Christianity. (Later, Italian Catholics used to refer to them as "Satan's horns" or "Lucifer's horns.") Pass the *corno* over the flame of a red candle to heat a person's magical armor.

The Corno Gobbo

The Corno Gobbo is a well-dressed hunchback in a suit and top hat. Sometimes, images and tokens depict the lower part of his body as the red *corno*. He is often shown holding a lucky horseshoe and making the sign of the *mano cornuta*, the "horned hand" gesture thought to ward off the *malocchio*. He provides good luck to gamblers and protection against the evil eye. If you need extra luck, rub the hump on his back. Pass his image over the flame of a gold candle to have success at gaming.

Cimaruta

Cimaruta means "sprig of rue." This folk charm is traditionally worn around the neck or hung over the bed of an infant to ward off the evil eye. The branch of the rue is divided into three stems, symbolizing the triple Goddess, because rue is one of the sacred herbs associated with Her. Several small charms dangle from the stems—for example, a hand, a sword, and a fish, each with its own meaning. The primary symbols are the moon, serpent, and key, representing the Goddess in Her triple form as Hecate (the key), Diana (the moon), and Proserpina (the serpent). Pass over the flame of a red candle to banish bad luck.

THE LUCK OF THE IRISH: SANDRA'S FAMILY TRADITIONS

Not long after Sandra and Kevin got married, he was doing some wiring in the basement and found a strange rock nestled in the beams near the ceiling. Upon closer inspection, they discovered a yellowed, faded piece of paper attached to it. In gorgeous script, it read:

Lump of Coal
Struck by lightning
In office and in the presence of undersigned
Sept 11, 1884 5:25 PM
J[illegible] Fallon

The belief was that lightning wouldn't strike twice in the same place, so keeping the stone in the house meant the house was safe from that danger. Many other things have found their way into the house to protect it and keep the good luck coming. Here are a few you can bring into your home, too. Bless these charms by passing them over the flame of a white candle, or inscribe the symbol into the candle to call on the luck of the Irish.

CANDLEMAS AND THE CROSS OF BRIGID

Sandra's husband, Kevin, was born the day after Candlemas (February 2), a day when Christians would bring their annual stock of candles to the church to have them blessed. This holy day occurs the day after Irish patron St. Brigid's feast day on February 1. The story goes that she converted a pagan chieftain to Christianity on his deathbed by telling him the story of Christ while weaving a four-armed cross out of rushes that had fallen from his bedding. But the symbol can be traced back before Christianity, to the Goddess of fire and the hearth, Brigid. Brigid is celebrated with flame in the form of bonfires or candles on the Witch's sabbat Imbolc, along with the returning warmth and promise of spring. Brigid's crosses are usually placed above doorways and windows to protect the home, allowing only good luck to come in and keeping out all manner of evil spirits. You can also don a Brigid's cross pendant, like the one Kevin wears in honor of the Goddess. Bless it by passing it over the flame of a white candle.

I'M LOOKING OVER A FOUR-LEAF CLOVER

Sandra: *I've been lucky enough to find a four-leaf clover in my own back-yard on Gallows Hill in Salem, Massachusetts. It's a rare find, estimated to be 1 in 10,000. For centuries, it was believed that finding a four-leaf clover bestowed luck and protection from evil spirits and would even grant the possessor the ability to see Witches, fairies, and other magical trouble-makers before they could cause any shenanigans. The four leaves repre-sent four blessings of abundance: health, wealth, fame, and the love of a faithful companion. To secure this kind of prosperity and good fortune for yourself without having to endlessly search patches of clover, carve the symbol into a white, green, or gold candle and carry or wear a coin or other charm with the symbol on it that has been passed over the candle's flame.*

THE HAG STONE/HOLEY STONE:
AN CLOC COSANTA

Sandra and Kevin run a coven called Elphame, which is named for the home of the elves. This magical land was believed to be visible by peering through the naturally formed hole in what is known as a "hag stone" or "holey stone," and the Irish phrase for these organic treasures is "*an cloc consanta.*" A rich lore spanning many cultures surrounds the powers of these rocks, including protection for sailors (tie the stone to the ship's mast to keep evil away from the vessel and the cargo), farmers (hang the stone from the ceiling of the stable to bless and protect the livestock), and lovers (use to not only attract a mate but also to be able to tell if lies were being told). Suspend the stone by a string and hold it over a white candle to bless it. Smaller stones can be worn as pendants, and larger ones can be hung in the home or business.

THE GOOD OL' LUCKY PENNY

Sandra: *My nana always said, "Find a penny, pick it up, and all the day you'll have good luck!" This particular rhyme was popular at a time when a penny could buy necessities, and my great-grandmother Delia probably taught my nana this little bit of magic. In ancient times, metals were valued and considered gifts from the Gods, which explains the development and adornment of coins. Money has always been equated with luck because having money helps fix many problems, and not having money causes even more.*

If you do find a penny, you can tuck it into a dish or tray and burn a gold or green candle for prosperity to magnify the luck. Many people believe finding a penny is a sign from someone they love who has crossed over, so you may wish to keep it next to a vigil candle, lit for someone you miss who would wish you well.

CHAPTER 11

ILLUMINATION:
Psychic Power and Divination

You know by now that a burning candle can generate more than light and heat, but it can also serve as more than a conduit for wishes, prayers, or spells. Many Witches use candles when they scry, which is derived from the Old English word *descry*, meaning "to reveal." The act of staring into something—a crystal ball, a black mirror, a roaring fire, a pool of water—to induce psychic vision is scrying, and a candle flame works just as well if you are open to it.

Scrying has long been used as a method of divination, a source of inspiration, and a form of spirit communication. Early Egyptians used both fire and water in their temples to commune with their Gods. The Celts often used crystals turned into scrying plates to peer into the future by torchlight. Even Nostradamus used water and a candle to generate the predictions that people still reference to this day.

FLAME SCRYING

The most ancient form of scrying involves staring into fire for a vision. You can imagine our tribal ancestors sitting around a bonfire, gazing into the dancing, blazing energy to divine where to seek their quarry. This practice has come to be called pyromancy, and covens of Witches still do it. Sandra shares: *Three seasons out of four, my coven meets outdoors, in our backyard sanctuary. One of our favorite things to do is scry into a fire we build in our huge iron cauldron. Fire scrying is a lot like something many of us remember doing when we were kids: lying on our backs in the grass, staring up at the clouds, and pointing out shapes to our friends.* The things you see in the fire can tell you a lot—about what lies ahead but also what is within your heart. When you are faced with difficult decisions, fire scrying can reveal the truth and show you which path to take.

When building a campfire is not feasible, this magic can be easily accomplished with the light of a candle instead. The first time you seek answers this way, you might feel a little weird, but trust the process. It may take a few tries to make sense of what you are seeing—not just with your physical eyes but also with your inner knowing.

There are several ways to scry with fire. The methods vary, but they can all yield transformative and empowering results.

BEGINNING CANDLE SCRYING

When you're getting ready for divination, there are several things to consider.

Time and Place

Your space should be clean and peaceful. Busy, high-traffic areas in your home or office are filled with distractions that will impede your ability to bond to the flame. Choose a place where you won't be disturbed for at least an hour so you won't feel rushed.

Atmosphere

Engage your senses: use incense you find calming, like lavender, sandalwood, or amber. You may want to decorate the space with objects that empower you. Leanne uses seashells and items that link her to the ocean; Sandra has a handmade pouch of specially chosen crystals, stones, and small talismans that boost psychic abilities. Set the tone with music that makes you feel relaxed (but not sleepy), or play sounds like a waterfall, ocean waves, or falling rain. Your choice of seating, as well as your clothing, should be comfortable.

Mind-set

Now that everything in your physical environment has been chosen with the intention of supporting a sense of serenity and well-being, it's time to calm your mind so you can reach a meditative state. You should sink into ease in your body. Breathe deeply until you feel present and your mind is settled, not agitated, nervous, racing, or feeling like you are disconnected from your surroundings.

Candle Communication Tips

Fire has a big personality. Think about the strong emotions associated with flames: passion, anger, even hatred. This is an element you want on your side. But to work with it, you need to show it respect. When beginning the process of candle scrying, safety is the most important consideration. Your candle should be placed in a heat-safe container, and of course, you should never leave burning candles unattended. Keep your face a safe distance away from the flame, and don't stare directly at the brightest part of its light—keep your eyes on the base of the flame to avoid any harm to your vision.

CANDLE SCRYING (A.K.A. LYCHNOMANCY): SINGLE-CANDLE METHOD

Set a single candle in front of you in a heat-safe holder. You may choose to anoint it with an oil specifically formulated to enhance psychic ability (see Resources in the Appendix). Light the candle, saying:

"Candlelight, burning bright,
Let me see, what should be,
Candle flame, help my aim,
As you burn, I will learn."

Focus on the base of the flame, and ask the flame to respond to your questions. When the flame grows and climbs, you know you have its attention. Focus on and ask one question at a time. Pay attention to the shapes, the movement, and the intensity of the flames.

The Flame Speaks

These are some traditional interpretations of the flame's actions:

Wavering back and forth: You should expect a change of circumstance.

Twists/spirals: Beware of secret plots. Be more selective with who you let into your inner circle.

Rising and falling: Do not proceed. Use extreme caution. There is danger in your path.

Burns brightly and does not waver: Good fortune will come.

Sputters: Disappointment is around the bend. It is time to let go of what is not working.

Bright point at the tip of the wick: Expect success, but if the point quickly fades, the success will be short-lived.

Strong, high flame: There is a lot of good energy on the way. Roadblocks are coming down, and positive change and happy results are ahead.

Small but steady flame: Keep to your course. The future is positive, but there may be a wait. Stay focused on your goal.

Slight, faint flame, flickering and winding: Something is not right; the timing could be off in your life or there are hidden reasons why a certain path is not the best course.

Tall flame that dances with frenzied energy: Success will come, but with difficulties. This is usually an indication that people are working in opposition to your goal. If your desire is worth fighting for, prepare and proceed.

Blue flame: A higher spirit is present. This could mean angelic beings have taken an interest and noticed the life path on which you are traveling.

A flickering flame that drops and then grows steadily to become strong: Benevolent spirits are watching over, protecting, and guiding you. This is a sign of success for the future and a positive answer to the question.

Loud popping and crackling: External forces are making a considerable impact; the strength of the flame dictates if these are working toward or against your desires. A sputtering candle that is in danger of going out means trouble. A strong flame that pops and cracks indicates your ability to overcome obstacles to reach your goal with a bit of help from allies.

If the flame weakens and dies, your question cannot be answered at this time. Many readers assume this means the answer is no, and in that moment, it may be the case. But instead of resigning yourself to that as fact, focus and meditate on your desired outcome. If you believe it is worth the effort, you may be able to fix what is not working and ask again at a later date. (Be sure to leave enough time for the shift to manifest; some things can change in a few days or a week, and other things may take more effort and time.)

If the candle doesn't light at all—barring physical defects—your outcome may fall outside of your control. Try again at another time with a different candle after reassessing your goal.

Leanne says: *I have used scrying not only for peering into the future but also for meditation and stress release. It helps me let go of the anxieties of the day. While peaceful music is playing, I gaze into the flame of a white candle, calling in the intuitive force of the moon. As the fire dances before me, I allow my body to relax and see my problems turning into smoke and fading away.*

CANDLE WAX READINGS (A.K.A. CARROMANCY)

Reading candle wax is similar to reading tea leaves, but instead of interpreting the symbols and messages formed by wet leaves inside a teacup, we look at the candle drippings. In the first approach, a spell candle, typically a tall pillar candle not enclosed in a glass container, is allowed to burn down into a dish or bowl large enough to catch all the wax. You then examine the cooled drippings to determine what challenges or obstacles might impact the desired outcome of the spell or gauge the likely level of success. Another, more active method has been done for centuries, in which the drippings of a candle are poured into a bowl of cool water, and you watch as the wax cools and solidifies into shapes.

In either case, before you read the wax, follow the preparation steps outlined earlier in this chapter: choose your time and place, create your desired atmosphere, and get into your mind-set. After you have done that, you can set your intention for the reading.

If you are using the first, more passive method, follow the instructions for the spell candle, and wait for it to burn down to read the drippings.

If you are using the following active approach, get a bowl of water. Like in a tea reading, where you want to use a pale cup to best see the shapes of leaves, choose a ceramic or glass bowl (metal or plastic bowls are not recommended) in stark contrast to the color of your candle: if you're using a white candle, choose a dark bowl, and vice versa. Leanne has even used a large seashell. The type of candle you should use depends on how many questions you want to ask and how long you plan to take to conduct the reading. If you are asking a single question, a smaller candle, like a tealight or taper, will work. If you have several questions, you may wish to use a votive or even a jar candle to allow more wax to build up.

Active Wax Reading Method

- Fill the dish with clean water. Sandra prefers spring water, but any clean water will do.
- The water must be cool or room temperature; otherwise, it may affect how the wax takes shape.
- Sit comfortably in front of a table holding the dish in your palms.
- Look into the water and take three deep breaths, releasing any stress or tension you may feel.

- As you light the wick, sit and focus on your intention and your first question.
- As the heat of the candle starts melting the wax, breathe in through your nose and out through your mouth.
- Carefully holding the candle over the bowl, let the wax drip into the water. Keep the bowl still, and do not touch the water. Allow the wax and water to work their magic.

When you are ready to begin reading, peer into the water and examine the drippings, watching as the shapes take form. Look at the figures and the movement of the floating wax bits. Singular masses of wax may look like letters, animals, objects, or numbers. Stand back and examine the drippings as an entire image. Do they form a whole picture? Allow your instinctive mind to decipher the formations. Stay open to different interpretations of the representations that appear.

Thoughts and impressions can change over time, which is why recording and keeping a divination journal is so important. What you see one day may look different in the future. If a number shows up in the wax, that may designate a day or date. We have both received numbers that indicated the dates of critical events years in the future, which is why recordkeeping is vital—we never would have been able to keep those details in our heads. Letters typically refer to the names of people or places. Circles often indicate the end of a cycle in a person's life. Many symbols that we have seen in our tea readings also show up in the wax. As we have always said, knowing the traditional meanings of the symbols is helpful, but be sure to focus on what the shapes mean to you. There is no wrong way to interpret them, and with practice, the symbols and shapes will be easier to recognize. The more your psychic ability is challenged and worked, the stronger the messages that come through.

SCRYING BY CANDLELIGHT

CANDLELIGHT MIRROR SCRYING

When you picture someone peering into a crystal ball or a black mirror, you generally don't imagine them doing it in broad daylight. A dark room lit only by candles sets the mood for divination and magic, and the flickering of a dancing flame makes it easy for even a beginner to achieve the trancelike state of mind that allows for the flow of psychic information. The flame acts as a focal point for visualization. Alongside a bowl of water, a mirror, a crystal ball, or any reflective surface, it becomes a window into another world.

CREATE YOUR OWN BLACK MIRROR

It's easy to create a black mirror for scrying. You need:

- ◆ Picture frame with glass intact (It doesn't have to be fancy; re-purpose one you already own, or pick one up at a thrift shop or dollar store.)

- ◆ Black acrylic paint and a paintbrush, or a piece of plain black cloth (fabric glue optional)

1. Carefully remove the backing from the frame.

2. Create a seamless black surface on the interior of the glass:

   a. If using paint, coat the interior side of the glass in broad strokes. Let the first coat dry before adding a second. When it's dry, hold it up to the light to be sure no gaps remain. If you see light through any spaces you missed, use the same broad strokes to fill them in. When there are no gaps and the paint is dry, place the glass paint–side in.

   b. If using black cloth, cut it to cover the interior of the backing of the frame. Smooth out any wrinkles. If you want to secure the cloth with fabric glue to stabilize it, only use glue on the outside of the backing, not the interior, because distracting marks may show through the fabric. The goal is a perfectly smooth, completely black surface.

3. Replace the backing in the frame.

Setting the Intention

Before you begin, set your intention for the reading. Do you want to peer into the future? Communicate with someone who has crossed over? View something happening remotely in the present? Receive visions from a past life? With patience and practice, you can use the black mirror to do any of these things.

Choose a candle that will aid your intention. A taper candle safely and securely placed in a holder is a solid choice, but a votive would work as well. A white candle can be charged for any purpose: choose meaningful symbols to carve into it, and anoint it with an appropriate oil (see Chapter 2 for guidance).

To begin the reading, place the candle on the table between you and the mirror. Close your eyes, and take three deep, cleansing breaths. Inhale through your nose and exhale through your mouth. Focus on your breathing, and let everything else go. Open your eyes and focus on the reflection of the flame of the candle in the mirror. Keep looking as long as you can without blinking. When you feel compelled to blink, keep your eyes closed a moment. You should still be able to see the candle flame in your mind's eye. If you cannot, open your eyes again and continue to gaze at the flame in the mirror until you can still visualize it with your eyes shut, so even when you slowly blink, you can see the flame. Open your eyes, and stare into your own reflection in the mirror. Your own image will begin to fade like a cloudy sky. In its place, you may see symbols, scenes, or even another face appear as yours fades away.

When the image in the mirror transforms, you are "seeing" with your psychic mind. As with all methods of divination, you should record your visions in a journal so you can refer to them later as events transpire. Keeping track of the messages helps you improve at interpreting your visions.

Leanne shares: *I remember the first time I sat down to scry using a mirror and candle. It was not long after my dear friend Shawn passed away. Sitting in the dark, I begged spirit to show me what I needed to know to move on and find peace. The shape of a familiar face appeared in the flames and shadows within the mirror. It was Shawn, raising one eyebrow to me. It looked as if he was saying with humor, "Hey there." I would love to say I handled the magical moment with grace and reverence, but I was not as prepared for it as I thought I was. I screamed and jumped back, rocking the table and knocking the candle over in the process. Hot wax went everywhere. I was a mess, crying. Despite my shock at the sudden appearance of my friend, that experience began my love of scrying.*

CHAPTER 12

LIGHT POURS IN:
Simple Methods to Create
Custom Spell Candles

S andra: *I fondly recall learning how to pour jar candles from my friend Kim; she and I poured jar after jar in her kitchen. I gave a ton of them away as gifts that Yule. But that was my only experience creating my own candles. (Rolling the beeswax sheet ones at the Topsfield Fair doesn't really count!)*

I have often said, "You don't have to be a master herbalist to be a Witch . . . but it helps to know one." I feel the same way about candle-making. We are thrilled to share the techniques we have learned from our favorite experts who supply our covens and our stores with spell candles.

If you would prefer to purchase these items, rather than creating them from scratch, check out the Resources section.

"LIGHT, FOR THOSE WHO PREFER THE DARK": VOTIVE CANDLE TUTORIAL BY SHANNON MARIE DAOUST

Sandra: *My first experience with Master Chandler Shannon Marie Daoust's Dark Candles was many years ago—the first time Leanne ever gave me a Yule gift, she included Shannon's votive candles. I loved the rich, dark colors and intoxicating scents. It was years later that we tapped her to provide the votive and pillar spell candles for Hex and Omen. I spoke with Shannon about what started her on her journey, and she told me about what's probably a common motivation: she wanted candles that better reflected her own experiences and moods. That is a key benefit to making your own—you can customize them to suit whatever you desire.*

I asked Shannon to walk me through her process, and this is her advice for beginners.

SIMPLE VOTIVE CANDLE METHOD

To make six personalized votive candles, you need:
   1 pound soy, coconut, or beeswax (see the Buying Guide)
   1 ounce fragrance oil (if you choose essential oils, first be
      sure they are safe to burn)
   6 3-inch wicks

Standard 2-inch votive silicone mold (usually makes 3
   candles at a time)
2 pots: 1 large stockpot and 1 candle pouring pot (or
   saucepan with a pour spout) that fits inside the large pot
Long spoon/spatula (for stirring)
Candy thermometer
Optional: candle dye in your choice of color, 7 drops to 1
   pound
Optional: herbs for your purpose, 1 pinch per candle (see
   the Appendix to choose)

Fill the stockpot halfway full with water. Place the pouring pot
inside, and add the wax to the pouring pot. (If you don't have a
candle pot, don't use your best saucepan. Use an old pot that can now
serve as your candle pouring pot.) Heat the wax to 190°F to 200°F,
carefully checking it with the candy thermometer. Add the dye if you
are coloring your candles. (One more pro tip: don't use crayons because they will clog your wick and can be toxic.) Blend well, add the
fragrance, and blend well again.

Pour the hot wax into the molds, filling them to about ¼ inch
below the top of each opening. Wait 3 minutes and then push a wick
into the center of each filled mold.

After the first pour has cooled some, if you are using herbs, you
can add a pinch to each filled mold before you begin the second pour.
Reheat your reserved wax from your first pour and fill the void (the
sink hole) in the candles until you reach the level of the first pour.
Poke relief holes around the wick of the candles after the wax has
become solid but is still pliable.

You want your second pour to be 10°F hotter than your first pour to minimize lines on the sides of the candles. Repeat the repour process as necessary. When the candles are cool, usually within 2 to 4 hours, you can remove them from the molds. You can then reheat the wax and repeat the process, using up the rest of the wax to make the other three votive candles. They will be ready to be prepared further or used as-is in your spellwork.

"MADE WITH A LITTLE MOON MAGIC": DEVOTIONAL PILLAR CANDLE TUTORIAL BY JUNE JENNINGS

Sandra: *One of my closest friends and a priestess in my coven, June Jennings of June's Wicked Wax, has created countless custom pillar candles for me. Her attention to detail and the care she takes are unparalleled. When it came time for Leanne to stock Pentagram, she jumped at the chance to have June create some of her magic for the store.*

There's an old saying in Witchcraft: "Guard the mysteries well; reveal them constantly." When I asked June to teach us her method, she was quick to share. Her graciousness and generosity permeate everything she does, which is one of the many reasons we have relied on her through the years. She has been making her own candles for personal use for the better part of 20 years. Where she lived at the time she started, no shops sold anything other than "normal" candles, so she decided to learn to make her own, using soda cans as molds at first.

DIVINELY INSPIRED

Although she has made dozens of custom pillars, June feels that each candle is different, even though she uses the same process to create them. Much like the Gods Themselves, she told us her candles are distinct and have their own individual vibes: "They have lives of their own and come out exactly how they want to." If you want to create your own devotional pillar candle, June recommends doing research on the God or Goddess you want to dedicate it to and then meditating to ask Them how They would like Their candle to look and smell.

DEVOTIONAL PILLAR CANDLE PROCESS

To make your large devotional pillar candle, you need:
1 pound coconut/paraffin wax blend (2 cups melted wax
    will make 1 3.5×6-inch pillar. See the Buying Guide.)
6 drops fragrance or essential oil per 2 cups (be careful
    choosing essential oils because some are unsafe to burn)
Wick pin and 8-inch wick
Standard 3.5×6-inch pillar silicone mold
2 pots: 1 large stockpot and 1 candle pouring pot (or
    saucepan with a pour spout) that fits inside the large pot
Long spoon/spatula for stirring
Candy thermometer
Optional: candle dye in your choice of color, 7 drops to
    1 pound

Optional: additional ingredients, up to and including dried
herbs, crystals, essential oils, shells, mica powder, or
glitter (see the Buying Guide)

Prep the mold with the oil you wish to use, and add whatever additional ingredients you have chosen that are associated with the deity you wish to honor.

Set your wick using the wick pin to create the hole that will later hold the actual wick. (Before the wax goes into the mold, a metal pin is set inside the mold to create the space the wick will go. When the candle is nearly cured, remove the pin and replace it with the wick.) The more centered the wick is, the more evenly the candle will burn.

Fill the stockpot halfway full with water, and place the pouring pot inside. Heat the coconut/paraffin wax blend on low (electric stoves) or the lowest flame (gas stoves). When the blend is liquefied, add any dye and stir once to blend, then add the fragrance and stir once. Simmer for at least an hour. The wax should be approximately 180°F.

After you pour the wax into the mold, the candle will need to cure for about an hour before you can remove the wick pin and put in the actual wick. After the wick is set, the candle should stay in its mold for up to 4 more hours. When it is fully cured, you can pop it out of the mold.

"HERBAL CREATIONS MADE WITH INTENTION": HAG CANDLE TUTORIAL BY JIM SAYER

Sandra: *When I was ready to help my coven say goodbye to the 2020 calendar year, I reached out to my friend Jim Sayer at House of Life Botanicals to request a custom order of his phenomenal hag candles. Part of Jim's family hails from Scotland and Ireland, and he has Shawnee roots as well; both branches have shared their traditions of folk magic as well as plant/herb wisdom with him, which gave birth to his life's work. Memories of his "mammaw" making her mullein flower stalks helped form his method for creating the mullein hag candles I knew would best help us banish all the negativity from the harrowing year so we could carry only the best energy with us into 2021.*

Jim lovingly describes the way he recalls his great-grandmother making the "Witch candles," teaching him to cut the mullein stalks after they bloomed in the fall. She would leave them to dry in the old barn alongside the tobacco leaves. Cutting them to about six to eight inches long, she would be sure to leave enough of the stem to hold onto, or to push into the ground, because they were used both ways. The final step was coating them in lard and then leaving them to dry in the cool root cellar.

Before electricity existed, mullein candles had practical and medicinal uses. Jim's mammaw would reach for a mullein torch to light her way to the barn at night to attend a sick animal. Dressed in healing herbs, the candle would serve as both light and remedy when someone was ill. She would light the candle, rub some of the same lard and herb mixture on the patient's chest and feet, and chant and pray. Jim has modernized the method a bit by using beeswax instead of animal fat, but the intention and the spirit of his family's tradition remain intact.

Hag candles can be used in spells for purifying a space, healing, banishing, and connecting with spirits (particularly ancestors); for protection; or as part of a sabbat ritual.

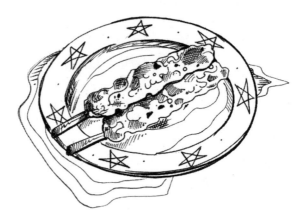

MULLEIN HAG CANDLES

MAKE YOUR OWN HAG CANDLE

To make mullein hag candles, you first have to grow or find mullein. It's a hardy plant, and you might see wild varieties growing by the roadside. If not, it's easy to grow in your garden. Some variety of mullein grows in the temperate seasons in most zones. Check one of the many online maps to see what zone you're in. As long as you're somewhere between zones 3 and 11, you can grow some form of mullein or find it in the wild near you.

Harvest stalks in the autumn after they've bloomed and when they've begun to go to seed. Cut the stalks to approximately 8 inches long, leaving enough of the stem to hold the stalk comfortably in your hand. Dry the stalks for a few weeks to ensure moisture won't cause molding.

Choose your herbs according to your intention, need, and correspondences, and create a blend that is tailored to your purpose. (See the Table of Correspondences on page 220 for guidance.)

When the stalks have dried, they're ready for candle-making.

You need:
> 4 to 6 dried mullein stalks
> 2 pots: 1 large stockpot and 1 candle pouring pot (or saucepan with a pour spout) that fits inside the large pot
> 2 cups beeswax pastilles
> 1- or 2-inch-wide paintbrush
> 2 sheets waxed paper
> Optional: herbs for your chosen intention
> Heat gun (see the Buying Guide)

Fill the stockpot halfway full with water. Place the pouring pot inside, and bring the water to a boil. Drop in beeswax, and melt until liquefied. Remove from the heat, and begin painting the wax all over the mullein stalks. As each layer is applied, lay the coated stalk on waxed paper to dry. When the candle is approximately 1½ inches thick and completely dry, you can add your herbs.

Using the heat gun (like those used for shrink wrap), warm small portions of the beeswax and push the herbs into the melted coating, shutting the gun off while doing so to avoid burning the herbs. Leave part of the top of the stem uncovered to make it easier to light; if you cover the entire tip with wax, you will need to melt it off for the torch to stay lit. This can be tedious work, so use the time to imbue your creation with your intention. Think about the purpose of the candle while heating it, and as you push in the herbs, picture the results you are hoping for.

When the candles are cooled, you can store them or keep on your altar until you need to use one.

HAG CANDLE ETIQUETTE

- Burn outdoors because the flame can grow as tall as 3 inches or more.
- Expect each torch to burn approximately 15 minutes per inch.
- Plan to burn all the way down, or douse the tip in water and then cut off the wet part to save the candle for later use.
- Burn in a heat-safe container, such as a cauldron filled with sand, or place in the ground.

Whenever we make something by hand, we place even more of our own energy into it, right from the start. The time and effort we invest in our own spell components add another layer of potency to them, and when we burn them, it is a true offering of a bit of ourselves to the spirits, the Gods, and the Universe.

AFTERWORD

From Sandra

"Nobody can tell me that magic isn't real."

Writing our first book, *Reading the Leaves,* was an incredible adventure that took us down a road we had never traveled. It taught us many important things about the world of publishing, and it gave us a way to connect with and teach many more people than our events ever could. In March 2020—just before the lockdown was announced—Leanne and I went to New York City to meet with the team at Penguin Random House to celebrate the upcoming launch of the book and host a tea leaf reading event with the press and influencers. Some people decided not to attend, but we had a wonderful, lively group of people with us that day, and everyone stayed safe despite the absence of things we now take as a daily part of life, like masks. We had so much fun interpreting the messages in everyone's cups, and all of us left feeling better about the future, despite the even-greater-than-usual uncertainty.

I remember looking around Times Square that night . . . that was my first time standing in it, and it was practically a ghost town. It felt surreal. Although we were overjoyed to be there, we sensed an undercurrent of disquiet. On the ride home, a friend warned me that we would soon all be asked to quarantine at home. I didn't want to believe it, but psychically I knew it to be true and felt the weight of it hit me: life as we knew it would be forever changed.

When it came time to begin our second book that autumn, we knew we had our cowriting method down to a science. This should have been an easier book to bring into the world. But life has a funny way of making sure you never get too comfortable.

Many months of the pandemic brought us significant challenges: feelings of isolation balanced against fear of exposure to the virus, with constant worry and stress leading to decision fatigue. I set up an entire altar in my temple devoted to healing, and I lit candles on it every single day without fail. Each morning I would begin the work on the coven's altar anew: one candle to shield people from the virus; one to help heal those who were already battling it; one to send strength, protection, and courage to all frontline workers; one to shore up everyone's financial health; and one to help the scientists discover how to beat the virus—with the request that they share all aid willingly and selflessly. Every day we quarantined at home, we hosted a Tea Time gathering online for all like-minded people, teaching about stones, herbs, and other Witchcraft-related topics. It kept us from feeling disconnected, and it reminded us of how linked we all truly are.

I have never in my life burned through so many candles in such a short period, so when it came time to write *Lighting the Wick*, I was more than ready to share what I felt had been my number one method of fighting the unseen foe that was threatening to destroy our way of life. Despite feeling eager to express, it was a struggle to deliver, for both of us. We talked (and felt better that we were each feeling the same way) and made a game plan to overcome the obstacles with the help of candles, crystals, and communication. Once we broke through the blocks, each chapter came together with the same magic we experienced the first time around. We were writing the chapters out of order, and one in particular had such a tremendous impact, it gave birth to this Afterword: Chapter 10, the one about luck.

Leanne decided she would write about her devotion to Fortuna, and I wanted to honor my patron, Ganesha. He is a god of luck, but that wasn't typically how I thought of Him. Humility, wisdom and intellect, prosperity and generosity, recordkeeping, spiritual power, and, yes, removing (and placing) obstacles were all instant, deeper associations for me. But His link to luck is solid. He is worshiped at the start of any prayer, and He is honored to bless new beginnings. Leanne also shared a spell she learned when she was in one of her favorite lucky destinations: Las Vegas.

In the 36 hours following the completion of Chapter 10, two things happened. The first one I cannot share here, as I am a big believer in keeping secrets until it is the right time to reveal them. The other is that a secret was finally revealed to me—a mystery I had been waiting my entire life to solve.

Magic and science may be two sides of the same coin, and in some ways, magic is science we haven't quite figured out yet. It was the combination of the two that gave me an incredible gift: a half-sister, the first blood relative I've ever known. She had reached out to me based on DNA data—my first "close family" match. My husband had given me the kit for Yule two years prior, and thus far, no one had come any closer than possible cousins. The minute I saw her face, our link was undeniable. This was the first time I had ever looked into the face of another person to see my own features reflected there. I cannot express how profound that feeling was for me; I suspect most of you reading this have taken this for granted your whole lives. If you're adopted like me, and if you've found your birth family, you know what I'm talking about. The timing of her appearance was mind-blowing enough but then I found out where she's been living for most of her life: *Las Vegas!*

She brought another piece of the puzzle with her: the identity of my birth father, from whom I definitely get my looks, alpha energy, and entrepreneurial spirit. At the time of this writing, we have not yet decided if we will contact him. I know I'll be guided to do what will be best for all of us: I will brew a cup of tea, light a candle, and ask Ganesha to bring us all good luck.

ACKNOWLEDGMENTS

From Both of Us

Joy Tutela, we are so blessed to have your continuing support and guidance. Thinking back to our meetings at Breaking Grounds Café, we are living proof of their motto: "Changing lives, one cup at a time." You've changed ours for the better, and we're eternally grateful.

Nina Shield, Lauren Appleton, Hannah Steigmeyer, Dorian Hastings, Laura Corless, Jess Morphew, Danielle Deschenes, Farin Schlussel, Carla Iannone, Marlena Brown, Marian Lizzi, Anne Kosmoski, Megan Newman, Christy Wagner, and the entire TarcherPerigee/Penguin Random House team, we cannot express how much your efforts mean to us. This is our dream, and you are a big part of it. A thousand thank-yous.

Lisa Ainsworth, once again you have brought our visions to life in these pages. Thank you for being our Empress of Ink!

June Jennings, Shannon Marie Daoust, and Jim Sayers: thank you for sharing your maker magic with us. What you do is so incredibly vital—to Witchcraft and the world—and we are proud to help pass the torch to others who will keep the methods alive.

To all the owners and buyers of stores carrying *Reading the Leaves*, and all the readers who purchased it, this new book is here because you believed in us. We will be forever grateful.

To Sgt. Timothy H., thank you for the support (and your service); we and our fans look forward to the next book jacket video!

To the Gods!

From Sandra

Kevin, you're my favorite fire-starter. You are the hearth in our home where we have forged so many of our dreams, and they keep getting bigger and better. All my love, always.

Elphame: Kevin, Deb, Leslie, June, Russell, and Michael, thank you for tending the flame.

My band, Go Your Own Way, thank you for helping to keep me sane through the pandemic. *Never Break the Chain!*

Leanne, Robin Benway said the only thing stronger than magic is sisterhood. We have both! I am so proud of everything we have done, and I look forward to our next adventures. We continue to *Break Every Box* because we were *Born To Do This.*

From Leanne

Tim Reagan, thank you for illuminating the mysteries of candle magic for me. You inspired much of my writing. Because of you, I possess a light within that will never die.

Much gratitude to Taliesin, for helping me remember whose daughter I was and making sure my crown was on straight. Thank you for everything you did to support me during the creation of this book.

My favorite, Amanda Bryant-McIntyre, thank you for enlightening me regarding the gifts of Fire. May you always burn bright.

Maelona, thank you for shining your knowledge and healing light. You were a huge help assisting me in creating a healing flame to light the wick of my creativity.

Danielle Tracey, thank you for the love and fiery passion you gave to this book. You are my daily dose of ylang-ylang!

Sandra, thank you for having the confidence to trust me with your dream. You have empowered me to reach for the stars. You have reminded me that "I was born to do this." Our friendship has not only transformed me but has helped others grow, too. The magic we do breaks boxes. Here we are, doing it again.

APPENDIX

RESOURCES: BUYING GUIDE

GALLOWS HILL WITCHERY

www.facebook.com/gallowshillwitchery

Sandra and Kevin Wright run Gallows Hill Witchery from their home at the top of Gallows Hill in Salem, Massachusetts, featuring a gorgeous selection of sterling silver jewelry and talismans, palm stones, crystal wands, spheres, and skulls, and Sandra's "Banish and Bless" incense. Sandra hosts live sales on Facebook for her "Crystal Coven," and creates successful vendor events via her company Spirit Beacon: Psychic Fair and Mystical Marketplace.

PENTAGRAM: WITCHCRAFT AND MAGICK SHOPPE

www.pentagramsalem.com

Witches Leanne Marrama and Timothy Reagan welcome you to Pentagram: Witchcraft and Magick Shoppe, a place where magick is for everyone! Sample their wares and authentic goods, including candles, incense, potions, and jewelry. Many of the items are handcrafted by real practicing Witches.

HEX: OLD WORLD WITCHERY

www.hexwitch.com

Whether you want a handmade candle to bless your home, herbs to mix up your own magic, a real love potion, books on the arts of Witchery, or a Voodoo doll crafted by a true practitioner, Hex is for those who believe in magic and those whose hearts beat with its fire.

OMEN PSYCHIC PARLOR & WITCHCRAFT EMPORIUM

www.omensalem.com

Pure essential oils, sacred incense from distant lands, crystal bath bombs, handmade amulets and talismans, and a trove of genuine stones and crystals.

WICKED WAX

https://www.etsy.com/shop/JunesWickedWax

As proprietress of Wicked Wax Candles, June is a master of her craft. She creates handcrafted devotional and intention candles during the most auspicious moon phases and planetary alignments. You can find her magickal candles on her website and in select stores in Salem, Massachusetts.

DARK CANDLES

www.darkcandles.com

With an outstanding record of great customer service and superior products, Dark Candles is committed to providing unique candles, body care, and home fragrance for people like us—those who have a penchant for the macabre and the darker side of life, all year long!

THE HOUSE OF LIFE BOTANICALS

www.thehouseoflifebotanicals.com

The House of Life Botanicals is a small-batch apothecary, creating handcrafted herbal offerings with intention for personal wellness: body, mind, and spirit.

INTENTION	COLOR	DAY OF THE WEEK	OIL	HERB	
Candles Radiate Warmth: Friendship, Love, Passion, and Cooperation					
Attraction	Red, Blue	Friday	Cinnamon, Ginger, Ylang–ylang, Almond	Cinnamon, Clove, Damiana, Ginger, Ylang–ylang, Jasmine	
Cooperation	Yellow, Pink	Friday, Wednesday	Lemon, Passion flower, Calendula	Catnip, Dandelion, St. John's wort, Olive leaf	
Breaking Up	Black	Saturday	Black pepper	Sage, Rosemary, Sea salt	
Friendship	Green, Orange, Pink, White, Yellow	Friday	Lemon, Passion flower, Sweet pea	Lemon, Mullein, Passion flower, Pink roses	
Infidelity	Black, White	Saturday	Ylang–Ylang	Chickweed, Clover, Elder, Licorice, Rhubarb, Rosemary, Walnut, Cayenne, Black pepper	
Kindness	Pink, Yellow	Sunday	Lavender, Lemon, Meadowsweet, Rose, Vanilla	Vanilla, Rose	
Love	Pink, Green	Friday	Bergamot, Clary sage, Ylang–ylang	Basil, Calendula, Oregano, Patchouli, Thyme, Rose	
Passion	Red, Pink	Tuesday	Cinnamon, Ginger, Ylang–ylang, Jasmine	Cinnamon, Clove, Cumin, Dill, Garlic, Jasmine, Mint, Orchid, Saffron	
Pets	Brown	Friday, Sunday	Rosemary, Vanilla	Rose, Rosemary	
Making Up	Green, Pink, Yellow, White, Blue	Sunday	Honey, Jasmine, Sandalwood, Vanilla	Sage, Rosemary, Salt	
Self–Love	Green	Friday	Lavender	Lavender, Patchouli, Pink roses	
Sex and Lust	Red	Tuesday	Cinnamon, Ginger, Ylang–ylang, Almond, Jasmine	Cinnamon, Clove, Damiana, Ginger, Ylang–ylang, Jasmine	

STONES	SYMBOLS TO CARVE	ZODIAC SIGNS	PLANETS	TAROT CARD	CHAKRA
Garnet, Carnelian, Ruby	Symbols for Mars and Venus	Leo, Libra	Venus, Sun	Empress	Heart, Root
Carnelian, Unakite, Rutilated quartz	Peace sign	Gemini, Virgo	Mercury	Three of Cups	Crown
Black tourmaline, Jet, Smoky quartz	Broken heart	Capricorn	Saturn	Tower	Crown
Emerald, Lapis lazuli, Rose quartz	Heart, Infinity	Libra, Taurus	Venus	Three of Cups	Heart
Black tourmaline, Jet, Smoky quartz	Broken Heart	Capricorn	Saturn	Tower	Root
Rose quartz, Aventurine	Heart, Peace	Cancer, Libra, Pisces	Moon, Venus	Two of Cups	Heart
Rose quartz, Chrysoprase,	Heart	Libra, Taurus	Venus	Lovers	Heart, Root, Throat
Carnelian, Clear quartz, Garnet	Genitalia	Leo, Scorpio	Mars, Sun	Ace of Wands	Heart, Root
Tiger's-eye, Labradorite	Heart, Infinity	Pisces, Cancer	Moon, Mercury	Queen of Cups	Heart
Rhodochrosite, Rose quartz, Obsidian, Amethyst	Peace sign, Heart	Libra, Cancer	Venus	Two of Cups	Crown, Heart, Throat
Amazonite, Aventurine	Heart, Infinity	Leo	Sun	Sun	Crown
Carnelian, Garnet, Red jasper	Genitalia	Leo, Libra, Scorpio	Mars, Sun, Venus	King of Wands	Root

INTENTION	COLOR	DAY OF THE WEEK	OIL	HERB	
Fiery Wall of Protection: Banish the Bad Stuff					
Banishing	Black, White	Saturday	Cedarwood, Geranium, Sage, Sandalwood	Camphor, Rosemary	
Fiery Wall of Protection	Red	Tuesday	Bay, Citronella, Pine	Bay leaf, Fennel, Rosemary, Rue, Kosher salt	
Four Guardians Candle Spell	Black	Saturday	Rosemary	Kosher salt, Sage	
Protection	Black, Red, White	Tuesday, Saturday	Cedarwood, Juniper, Olive, Rosemary	Garlic, Lavender, Palo santo, White sage, Rosemary	
Protection Jar	Black, Red	Saturday, Sun	Vinegar, Rosemary	Bay leaf, Garlic, Rosemary, Rue, Sea salt	
Return to Sender	Black	Saturday	Black pepper, Tabasco sauce	Clove, Red pepper flakes	
St. Michael— Protection	Red	Sunday	Frankincense, Olive, Orange	Lavender, Red flowers, Thyme	
Shield	White	Daily	Frankincense	Frankincense, Lavender	
Stop Gossip	Black	Saturday	Clove, Olive	Clove, Sea salt	
Warding	Black, Red, White	Tuesday, Saturday	Clove, Fennel, Frankincense	Lavender	
Keeping the Lights On: Career Concerns and Money Mojo					
Business	Blue, Gold, Green, Yellow	Thursday, Sunday	Allspice, Basil, Bergamot, Grapefruit, Ginger, Honeysuckle	Basil, Bay leaf, Patchouli	
Career Confidence	Blue, Yellow, Gold	Thursday, Sunday	Basil, Olive, Patchouli	Basil, Bay leaf, Patchouli	
Cash Flow	Gold, Green, Yellow	Sunday	Basil, Ginger	Nutmeg, Pine	

STONES	SYMBOLS TO CARVE	ZODIAC SIGNS	PLANETS	TAROT CARD	CHAKRA
Black tourmaline, Jet, Smoky quartz	Shield	Capricorn, Aquarius	Saturn	Tower	Crown
Ruby, Carnelian, Red jasper, Garnet, Fire agate	Shield	Aries	Mars	Temperance	Third Eye
Iron, Tiger's-eye	Shield, Sword	Aries	Mars	Strength	Solar Plexus
Amethyst, Angelite, Black tourmaline, Hematite, Jade	Shield, Sword	Aries	Mars, Saturn	Queen of Swords	Solar Plexus
Iron, Tiger's-eye	Shield, Sword	Scorpio	Saturn	Justice, Queen of Swords	Solar Plexus
Black tourmaline, Jet, Smoky quartz	Shield	Gemini	Mercury, Saturn	Queen of Swords	Root
Black obsidian, Clear quartz	Sword	Leo	Sun	Sun	Solar Plexus
Black obsidian, Jet, Smoky quartz	Shield	Aries	Mars	King of Wands	Solar Plexus
Black tourmaline, Blue kyanite	Tongue	Gemini, Libra	Mercury, Saturn	Ace of Swords	Throat
Amber, Black tourmaline, Ruby	Shield	Aries	Mars	Strength	Crown
Aventurine, Citrine, Clear quartz	Arrow up	Taurus, Virgo	Venus	Ace of Pentacles	Root
Citrine, Sunstone	Arrow up	Leo	Sun	Strength	Solar Plexus
Malachite	Dollar sign	Libra	Venus	Nine of Pentacles	Solar Plexus

INTENTION	COLOR	DAY OF THE WEEK	OIL	HERB	
Career Guidance	Royal blue, Royal purple	Thursday	Orange, Rosemary	Basil, Rosemary	
Debt	Black, Gold, Green	Saturday	Basil, Frankincense	Basil, Sage, Sea salt	
Major Purchase	Blue, Gold, Green, Yellow	Wednesday, Thursday, Sunday	Patchouli, Basil, Olive	Basil, Calamus, Patchouli	
Money	Gold, Green, Yellow	Sunday	Allspice, Basil, Bergamot, Grapefruit, Ginger, Honeysuckle	Nutmeg, Pine	
Money Wheel	Gold, Green, Yellow, Royal blue	Thursday, Sunday	Bergamot, Orange	Basil, Chamomile, Cinnamon, Cinquefoil, Nutmeg	
Planetary Business Blessings					
Sunday	Yellow, Gold	Sunday	Citrus	Lemon leaf	
Monday	Lilac, Silver	Monday	Rose	Milk thistle, Rose	
Tuesday	Red	Tuesday	Cinnamon	Nettle, Black pepper	
Wednesday	Orange	Wednesday	Honeysuckle	Meadowsweet, Honeysuckle	
Thursday	Royal blue	Thursday	Jasmine	Comfrey, Jasmine	
Friday	Green	Friday	Vanilla	Hibiscus, Red raspberry	
Saturday	Black	Saturday	Olive	Poppy, St. John's wort	
Success	Black, Gold, Green	Thursday, Sunday	Basil, Frankincense, Olive	Basil, Cinquefoil, Nutmeg	
Quick Money	Gold, Orange, Yellow	Wednesday, Sunday	Bay, Citronella, Pine	Bay leaf, Garlic, Rosemary, Rue, Kosher salt	
Your Glow Up: Ignite Health and Well-Being					
Emotional	White, Silver, Lilac	Monday, Friday	Frankincense, Lavender	Lavender, Mugwort	
Everyday Candle Magic					
Sunday	Gold, Yellow	Sunday	Chamomile, Frankincense	Laurel, Marigold, Yellow roses, Sunflower	

STONES	SYMBOLS TO CARVE	ZODIAC SIGNS	PLANETS	TAROT CARD	CHAKRA
Amethyst, Labradorite	Sun	Leo	Sun	Strength	Solar Plexus
Black obsidian	Circle around dollar sign	Capricorn	Saturn	Six of Pentacles	Base
Jade, Pyrite	Dollar sign	Taurus	Venus	Ten of Pentacles	Base
Aventurine, Pyrite	Dollar sign	Leo, Libra, Taurus	Sun, Venus	Ace of Pentacles	Solar Plexus
Citrine, Pyrite, Tiger's-eye	Dollar sign	Leo	Sun	Ace of Pentacles	Solar Plexus
Citrine	Sun	Leo	Sun	Sun	Solar Plexus
Moonstone	Moon	Cancer	Moon	Moon	Third Eye
Carnelian	Symbol of Mars	Aries	Mars	The Emperor	Manipura
Moldavite	Symbol of Mercury	Gemini	Mercury	Magician	Throat
Lepidolite	Symbol of Jupiter	Sagittarius	Jupiter	Wheel of Fortune	Sacral
Aventurine	Symbol of Venus	Libra, Taurus	Venus	Empress	Heart
Black obsidian	Symbol of Saturn	Capricorn	Saturn	Seven of Pentacles	Third Eye
Aventurine, Citrine, Sunstone	Arrow up	Sagittarius	Jupiter	Six of Wands	Root
Pyrite	Dollar sign	Leo	Sun	Queen of Wands	Base
Moonstone	Yin and yang	Cancer	Moon	Queen of Cups	Heart
Sunstone	Sun	Leo	Sun	Sun	Solar Plexus

INTENTION	COLOR	DAY OF THE WEEK	OIL	HERB	
Monday	Silver, Lilac	Monday	Jasmine, Eucalyptus	Camphor, Jasmine, Wintergreen	
Tuesday	Red	Tuesday	Dandelion, Ginger	Bloodroot, Dragon's blood, Peppermint	
Wednesday	Orange	Wednesday	Lavender, Bergamot	Marjoram, Star anise, Sandalwood	
Thursday	Blue	Thursday	Clove, Sage	Agrimony, Pine	
Friday	Green	Friday	Sandalwood, Strawberry	Cardamom, Rose, Spearmint	
Saturday	Black	Saturday	Myrrh, Patchouli	Cassia, Poppy, Patchouli	
Healing Bath	Green, Pink, White	Monday	Lavender, Oregano, Vanilla	Lemongrass, Oregano, Rose	
Health Emergencies	White	As needed	Clove, Eucalyptus, Peppermint, Frankincense, Lemon, Tea tree	Clove, Lemon leaf, Peppermint, Sandalwood	
Healthy Weight	Light purple, White, Silver	Monday	Frankincense, Lemon	Dill, Green tea, Rosemary	
Morning Magic	Pink, White	Every day	Bergamot	Camphor, Eucalyptus, Lavender, Rose	
Physical	Green, Orange, Red	Wednesday, Friday, Sunday	Almond, Frankincense	Apple blossom, Chamomile	
Planned Procedures	White	As needed	Lime, Frankincense	Calendula, Ginger	
Pregnancy	Green, Silver	Monday, Friday	Lavender, Sandalwood, Orange, Lemon, Grapefruit	Fenugreek, Ginger, Peppermint, Rosehip	
Recovering	Green, Orange, Red	Friday, Sunday, Tuesday	Frankincense, Sandalwood	Camphor, Mint	
Relaxation	White, Silver, Lilac	Monday	Lavender	Chamomile, Thyme	
Spiritual	Silver, Lilac	Monday	Frankincense	Mullein, Olive leaf, Peppermint	

STONES	SYMBOLS TO CARVE	ZODIAC SIGNS	PLANETS	TAROT CARD	CHAKRA
Moonstone	Moon	Cancer	Moon	Ace of Cups	Sacral
Red jasper	Fire	Aries	Mars	Ace of Wands	Root
Blue lace agate	Sword	Gemini	Mercury	Ace of Swords	Throat
Lepidolite	Bow and arrow	Sagittarius	Jupiter	Emperor	Root
Aventurine	Heart	Taurus	Venus	Empress	Sacral
Yellow sapphire	Snake	Aquarius	Saturn	Star	Third Eye
Aventurine, Clear quartz, Moonstone	Dove	Cancer, Taurus	Moon, Venus	Queen of Cups	Sacral
Bloodstone, Fluorite, Selenite	Fire	Leo	Sun	Sun	Root
Amethyst, Moonstone, Iolite	Desired weight	Cancer	Moon	Moon	Sacral
Sunstone	Sun	Leo	Sun	Sun	Sacral
Amethyst, Smoky quartz, Red jasper	Tree	Virgo	Mercury	Temperance	Solar Plexus
Aventurine	Tree	Libra, Taurus	Venus	Hermit	Heart
Malachite, Moonstone, Rose quartz	Plus	Cancer, Taurus	Moon, Venus	Empress	Sacral
Bloodstone, Fluorite, Selenite	Snake wrapped around rod	Aries, Sagittarius	Jupiter, Mars	Four of Wands	Sacral
Amethyst, Moonstone, Rose quartz	Dove	Taurus	Venus	Four of Swords	Solar Plexus
Amethyst, Sodalite	Lotus	Cancer	Moon	The High Priestess	Soul Star

INTENTION	COLOR	DAY OF THE WEEK	OIL	HERB	
Lighting the Way Back: Breaking Bad Habits and Addictions					
Addictions	Black	Saturday (as needed)	Banishing, Frankincense	Rosemary, Sea salt	
Alcohol	Black	Saturday	Peppermint, Chamomile	Chamomile, Peppermint, Sage, Sea salt	
Banish Bad Habits	White	Saturday	Rosemary	Sandalwood	
Drugs	Black, Red, White	Saturday	Citrus	Nettle, Sea salt	
Food	White	Friday	Cinnamon	Sea salt	
Gambling—St. Bernardine	White	Saturday	Lemon	Cedar, Fennel, Thyme	
Love	Black, White	Saturday	Juniper, Vinegar	Kosher salt, Myrrh	
Smoking	Black	Saturday	Citrus, Peppermint	Catnip, Black cohosh, Blue vervain, Peppermint	
In Memoriam: Mediumship and Vigil Candles					
Ancestors	Black	Sunday	Frankincense, Myrrh	Frankincense, Mullein, Pipe tobacco	
Archangels					
Michael	Gold, Red	Sunday	Frankincense, Lemon, Tea tree	Anise, Ginger, Pine, Rosemary	
Gabriel	Orange	Monday	Eucalyptus, Jasmine	Myrrh, Rose	
Raphael	Yellow	Wednesday	Bergamot, Lavender, Mint	Bergamot, Lavender, Thyme	
Uriel	Blue	Thursday	Basil, Sandalwood	Basil, Ginger, Sandalwood	

STONES	SYMBOLS TO CARVE	ZODIAC SIGNS	PLANETS	TAROT CARD	CHAKRA
Amethyst, Citrine, Rose quartz	Broken links	Aquarius	Saturn	Devil	Solar Plexus
Amethyst, Carnelian, Hematite	The Word *Alcohol*	Capricorn	Saturn	Devil	Solar Plexus
Smoky quartz	Pentacle, Positive words	Capricorn	Saturn	Queen of Swords	Solar Plexus
Amethyst, Red jasper, Smoky quartz	Initials	Aquarius	Saturn	Star	Sacral
Gaspeite, Howlite, Iolite, Shungite	Initials, Venus, Symbol for Libra	Libra	Venus	Star	Root
Amethyst, Selenite, Smoky quartz	The Words *Strength* and *Courage*	Aquarius, Capricorn	Saturn	Star	Sacral
Black obsidian, Lepidolite	The Words *I love me more*	Aquarius, Capricorn	Saturn	Star	Sacral
Amethyst, Citrine, Peridot	No Smoking sign	Aquarius	Saturn	Ace of Swords	Throat
Amethyst, Lapis lazuli	Initials of ancestors	Capricorn	Saturn	Death	Third Eye
Amber, Sugilite	Sword	Leo	Sun	Sun	Third Eye
Aquamarine, Moonstone, Selenite	Trumpet	Scorpio	Mars	Ace of Cups	Third Eye
Aventurine, Citrine, Malachite	Eagle	Aquarius	Saturn	Death	Third Eye
Hematite, Obsidian, Rutilated quartz	Serpent	Sagittarius	Jupiter	The Hierophant	Third Eye

229

INTENTION	COLOR	DAY OF THE WEEK	OIL	HERB	
Automatic Writing	Black, White	Monday, Saturday	Frankincense	Patchouli, Spikenard, Wormwood	
Guardian Angel	White	Sunday	Frankincense, Myrrh	Angelica, Lavender	
Memorial Candles	Black, White	Monday, Saturday	Frankincense, Myrrh	Bay laurel, Mugwort	
Pendulum	Black, White, Silver	Saturday	Frankincense, Myrrh	Angelica, Dragon's blood, Wormwood	
Scrying Mirrors	Black	Saturday	Frankincense, Mugwort, Myrrh	Angelica, Cypress, Dragon's blood, Wormwood	
Séance	Black, White	Monday, Saturday	Clary sage, Frankincense, Mugwort	Lavender, Mugwort, Myrrh	
Shrine of Remembrance	Black, White, Yellow	Saturday	Mugwort	Patchouli, Spikenard	
Spirit Animals	Brown, White	Sunday	Frankincense, Myrrh	Acacia, Dragon's blood	
Spirit Boards	Black, White	Saturday	Patchouli, Mugwort	Angelica, Dragon's blood, Wormwood	
Spirit Guides	White, Purple	Monday	Frankincense, Mugwort	Mugwort, Myrrh	
Vigil	Black, Purple, Yellow, White	Saturday	Frankincense	Bay laurel, Cypress, Tobacco	
Let It Shine: Brilliant House Blessings					
Better Sleep	Purple, Silver, Deep blue, Indigo, White	Monday	Mugwort, Lavender	Catnip, Celery seed, Chamomile, Frankincense, Gardenia, Lavender, Mugwort, Valerian	

STONES	SYMBOLS TO CARVE	ZODIAC SIGNS	PLANETS	TAROT CARD	CHAKRA
Amethyst, Clear quartz, Lapis lazuli, Moonstone	Skull	Scorpio	Saturn	Death	Third Eye
Amethyst, Angelite, Moonstone	Angel wings	Cancer	Moon	Ace of Cups	Third Eye
Labradorite, Rose quartz	Skull	Aquarius, Cancer	Moon, Saturn	Chariot, Death	Third Eye
Moonstone	Eye	Cancer	Moon	Chariot	Third Eye
Amethyst, Clear quartz, Labradorite	Eye	Cancer	Moon, Saturn	Ace of Cups	Third Eye
Amethyst, Clear quartz, Lapis lazuli, Moonstone	Skull	Scorpio	Saturn	Death	Third Eye
Lapis lazuli, Moonstone, Rose quartz	Heart, Initials of beloved dead	Cancer	Moon	Ace of Cups	Third Eye
Serpentine	Animal's name	Taurus	Venus	King of Pentacles	Root
Amethyst, Clear quartz, Labradorite	Skull	Aquarius	Saturn	Death	Third Eye
Angelite	Angel wings	Sagittarius	Jupiter	Temperance	Third Eye
Labradorite	Name of beloved dead	Scorpio	Saturn	Death	Third Eye
Amethyst, Aquamarine, Moonstone, Opal, Clear quartz, Sandstone, Selenite, Turquoise	The word Zzzz	Cancer	Moon	Four of Swords	Crown

INTENTION	COLOR	DAY OF THE WEEK	OIL	HERB	
Blessing a New Home	Black, White	Saturday	Frankincense, Lavender, Myrrh, Sandalwood	Dragon's blood, Kosher salt, Sage	
Cleansing an Old Home	Black, White	Saturday	Anise, Rosemary	Kosher salt, Rosemary, Sage, Lavender	
Entertaining Company	Green, Orange, Pink	As needed	Rose, Vanilla	Marjoram, Rose	
Happy Home	Yellow, White	Sunday	Lemon, Citrus	Lemon balm, Rose, St. John's wort	
Kitchen Magic	Yellow	Sunday	Apple, Honeysuckle	Basil, Rose	
Memorial Dinner	Black, White	Saturday	Frankincense, Lavender, Myrrh	Acacia, Cedarwood, Myrrh	
Prophetic Dreams	Purple, Silver, Deep blue, Indigo	Monday	Lavender	Lavender, Rose, Anise, Mugwort, Patchouli	
Protection	Black, Red, White	Tuesday, Saturday, Sunday	Bay, Frankincense	Calamus, Peppermint	
Restoring Peace	White, Green, Pink	Friday, Sunday	Keep the Peace, Lavender, Olive, Patchouli, Mugwort, Hyssop	Anise, Chamomile, Lavender, Mugwort, Patchouli, Rose	
Romantic Dinner	Pink, Red	Friday, Sunday	Rose	Damiana, Red rose	
Sex	Red	Tuesday, Sunday	Cinnamon	Cinnamon, Clove, Damiana	
Study and Productivity	Blue, Orange	Wednesday, Thursday	Citrus	Lemon balm, Peppermint, St. John's wort	
Unwanted Energy	Black, White	Saturday	Sage	Sage, Rosemary	
Washing Away a Bad Day	Black, White	As needed	Rosemary	Lavender, Sage, St. John's wort, Rosemary	

STONES	SYMBOLS TO CARVE	ZODIAC SIGNS	PLANETS	TAROT CARD	CHAKRA
Amethyst, Black tourmaline, Rose quartz	House	Taurus	Venus	Ace of Pentacles	Root
Clear quartz, Rose quartz, Smoky quartz	House	Taurus	Venus	Ace of Pentacles	Root
Amethyst, Bloodstone, Rose quartz	Smile	Libra	Mercury, Venus	Three of Cups	Heart
Sunstone	Happy Face	Leo	Sun	Sun	Heart
Aventurine	Heart	Taurus	Venus	Empress	Solar plexus
Amethyst, Labradorite, Lapis lazuli	Skull	Aquarius	Saturn	Death	Third Eye
Moonstone	Eye	Cancer	Moon	Queen of Cups	Third Eye
Black obsidian, Aventurine, Tiger's-eye	Shield	Aries	Mars	King of Wands	Solar Plexus
Clear quartz, Rose quartz	Peace sign	Libra	Mercury, Venus	Two of Cups	Crown, Heart
Carnelian, Garnet, Rose quartz	Heart	Taurus	Venus	King of Pentacles	Solar Plexus
Carnelian, Garnet, Rose quartz	Genitalia	Aries	Mars	Ace of Wands	Sacral
Fluorite, Hematite	The Words *Do it*	Gemini	Mercury	High Priestess	Crown
Black obsidian, Blue kyanite	The Words *Be gone*	Capricorn	Saturn	The World	Foot
Black tourmaline, Smoky quartz	The Words *I am okay*	Capricorn	Saturn	The World	Foot

INTENTION	COLOR	DAY OF THE WEEK	OIL	HERB	
The Future Looks Bright: Ignite Good Luck, and Burn Away the Bad					
Advantage	Indigo	Monday	Bergamot, Cinnamon	Bay leaf, Basil, Peppermint	
Career	Yellow, Blue	Sunday, Thursday	Almond, Citrus, Success, Solar	Chamomile, Cinnamon, Olive leaf, Peppermint	
Changing Luck	Black, White	Saturday	Olive	Kosher salt	
Cimaruta	Black, Red, White	Tuesday, Saturday	Olive, Rue	Oregano, Rue	
Corno/Cornicello	Red	Tuesday, Saturday	Olive, Rue	Rosemary, Rue, Sage	
Corno Gobbo	Red	Sunday	Citrus, Olive	Oregano, Rue	
Fast Luck	Green, Gold, Yellow	Sunday, as needed	Almond, Cinnamon, Citrus, Success, Solar	Bay leaf, Cinnamon, Linden leaf, Rue	
Fortuna—Goddess of Luck	Gold, Yellow	Sunday, Daily	Almond	Frankincense	
Four-Leaf Clover	Yellow, Gold, Green	Sunday	Cinnamon	Copal, Frankincense	
Ganesha—Lord of Obstacles	Red, Gold	Tuesday, Wednesday	Jasmine, Lotus	Holy basil, Marjoram	
Gambling	Gold, Green, Yellow	Sunday, as needed	Almond, Citrus, Success, Solar	Allspice, Clove, Orange, St. John's wort, Vetiver	
Hag Stone	Black	Saturday	Patchouli	Rosemary, Rue, Sage	
Improving Luck	White	Wednesday, Sunday	Rosemary, Rue	Chamomile, Wintergreen	
Legal	Orange	Wednesday	Cedar	Meadowsweet, Lady's Slipper, Rosemary	

STONES	SYMBOLS TO CARVE	ZODIAC SIGNS	PLANETS	TAROT CARD	CHAKRA
Aventurine	Moon	Cancer	Moon	Chariot	Solar Plexus
Citrine, Blue kyanite	Dollar sign, Key, Sun	Leo, Sagittarius	Sun, Jupiter	Sun	Solar Plexus
Aventurine, Amazonite, Carnelian	Dollar sign, Sun	Leo, Sagittarius	Sun, Jupiter	Wheel of Fortune	Solar Plexus
Black tourmaline	Key, Moon, Serpent	Capricorn, Cancer, Aries	Mars, Moon, Saturn	Strength	Root
Black obsidian, Blue kyanite	Arrow up, Dollar sign	Aries, Capricorn	Mars	King of Wands	Root
Citrine, Blue kyanite	Arrow up, Dollar sign	Leo	Sun	Sun	Root
Aventurine, Carnelian	Dollar sign, Sun	Leo	Sun	Wheel of Fortune	Solar Plexus
Aventurine, Citrine, Sunstone	Cornucopia	Leo	Sun	Wheel of Fortune	Solar Plexus
Pyrite	Four-leaf clover	Leo	Sun	Sun	Solar Plexus
Quartz crystal, Pyrite, Citrine	Ax to cut ties/ red tape and cut through obstacles, lasso/ loop to snare goals	All	Mercury	Magician, Wheel of Fortune, Ace of Pentacles, Eight of Wands	Root
Aventurine, Amazonite, Carnelian	Horseshoe	Leo	Sun	Sun, Ace of Pentacles, Wheel of Fortune	Solar Plexus
Jet	Eye	Aquarius	Saturn	Temperance	Root
Aventurine, Smoky quartz, Pyrite	Dollar sign, Sun	Leo, Sagittarius	Sun, Jupiter	Wheel of Fortune	Solar Plexus
Garnet, Lapis lazuli	Scales	Gemini, Libra	Mercury	Justice	Root

INTENTION	COLOR	DAY OF THE WEEK	OIL	HERB	
Lucky Penny	Yellow, Gold	Sunday	Peppermint	Chamomile, Cinnamon, Olive leaf, Peppermint	
Lucky 13	Gold, Yellow	Sunday	Frankincense	Basil, Peppermint	
Malocchio—The Evil Eye	Black, White	Christmas Eve, as needed	Olive	Salt	
Money	Green	Friday	Basil	Bay leaf, Basil, Peppermint	
Odds in Your Favor	Gold, Yellow	Sunday	Citrus, Success, Solar	Nutmeg, Rue, Vetivert	
Cross of Brigid	Blue, Red, Yellow, White	Tuesday	Chamomile, Rosemary	Dill, Red clover	
Riches	Blue, Green, Gold, Yellow	Sunday, Thursday	Cinnamon	Basil, Cinquefoil, Ginger	
St. Cayetano	Green	Sunday	Allspice, Orange	Pine, Vetiver, Rue	
Sex	Red	Tuesday	Cinnamon	Rose, Ylang–ylang	
Illumination: Psychic Power and Divination					
Candle Wax Reading	Contrasting color to the scrying bowl	Monday	Frankincense, Myrrh	Bay, Clary sage, Flax seeds	
Flame Scrying	Black, Indigo, White, Silver	Monday, Saturday	Copal, Frankincense	Anise, Milk thistle, Poppy	
Mirror Scrying	Black, White, Silver	Monday, Saturday	Frankincense, Myrrh	Lavender, Hibiscus, Marigold	
Pendulum	Black, Indigo, White, Silver	Monday	Frankincense, Myrrh	Gum arabic, Lavender, Nutmeg	
Tarot	Black, Indigo, White, Silver	Monday	Lavender, Frankincense, Myrrh	Meadowsweet, Nutmeg, Star anise	
Tea Leaf Reading	Black, Indigo, White, Silver	Monday	Frankincense, Myrrh, Thyme	Anise, Camphor, Eyebright	

STONES	SYMBOLS TO CARVE	ZODIAC SIGNS	PLANETS	TAROT CARD	CHAKRA
Citrine, Sunstone		Leo	Sun	Strength	Solar Plexus
Pyrite	*13*	Capricorn	Saturn	Wheel of Fortune	Solar Plexus
Black tourmaline	Eye	Capricorn	Saturn	Temperance	Root
Aventurine, Pyrite	Dollar sign, Sun	Libra, Leo, Taurus	Jupiter, Venus	Ace of Pentacles	Solar Plexus
Aventurine, Amazonite, Citrine	Dollar sign, the words *Good Luck* or *Windfall*	Leo	Sun	Wheel of Fortune	Solar Plexus
Citrine, Bloodstone	Fire	Aries	Mars	Strength	Root
Aventurine, Amazonite, Carnelian	Dollar sign, Sun	Leo, Sagittarius	Sun, Jupiter	Ace of Pentacles	Root
Aventurine	Dice	Libra, Taurus	Venus	King of Pentacles	Root
Carnelian	Genitalia	Aries	Mars	Ace of Wands	Root and Sacral
Labradorite, Moonstone, Fluorite	Moon	Cancer	Moon	Chariot	Third Eye
Amethyst, Moonstone, Quartz crystal	Moon	Cancer	Moon	Chariot	Third Eye
Amethyst, Moonstone, Quartz crystal	Moon	Cancer	Moon	Chariot	Third Eye
Labradorite, Moonstone, Fluorite	Moon	Cancer	Moon	Chariot	Third Eye
Amethyst, Moonstone, Quartz crystal	Moon	Cancer	Moon	Chariot	Third Eye
Amethyst, Moonstone, Quartz crystal	Moon	Cancer	Moon	Chariot	Third Eye

BIBLIOGRAPHY

Books

Buckland, Raymond. *Advanced Candle Magick: More Spells and Rituals for Every Purpose.* St. Paul, MN: Llewellyn Publications, 1996.

———. *Practical Candleburning Rituals: Spells and Rituals for Every Purpose.* 3rd ed. St. Paul, MN: Llewellyn Publications, 1982.

Crowley, Aleister, and Israel Regardie. *777 and Other Qabalistic Writings of Aleister Crowley.* York Beach, ME: Adfo Books, 1986.

Heldstab, Celeste Rayne. *Llewellyn's Complete Formulary of Magical Oils: Over 1200 Recipes, Potions & Tinctures for Everyday Use.* St. Paul, MN: Llewellyn Publications, 2012.

Melody, and Julianne Guilbault. *Love Is in the Earth: A Kaleidoscope of Crystals: The Reference Book Describing the Metaphysical Properties of the Mineral Kingdom.* 3rd ed. Wheat Ridge, CO: Earth Love Pub House, 1995.

Websites

Aayush. "15 Powerful Ganesha Mantras to Remove Obstacles & Achieve Success." Vedicfeed. July 21, 2020. https://vedicfeed.com/powerful-ganesh-mantras.

"Bedroom Magick—Sleep & Dreams." *Muse of Hestia* (blog). May 29, 2015. http://hestiashearthmuse.blogspot.com/2015/05/bedroom-magick-sleep-dreams.html.

Cameron, Yogi. "A Beginner's Guide to the 7 Chakras." mbg mindfulness. October 8, 2020. https://www.mindbodygreen.com/0-91/The-7-Chakras-for-Beginners.html.

Desy, Phylameana Iila. "How to Do a Candle Wax Reading." Learn Religions. June 25, 2019. https://www.learnreligions.com/candle-wax-reading-1729540.

"Manifesting Financial Success: Herbal Correspondences in Money Magick." Witch Swap. February 24, 2020. https://www.witchswap.com/blog/manifesting-financial-success-herbal-correspondences-in-money-magick.

"Orphic Hymn to Tyche." Hellenion.org. (n.d.). https://www.hellenion.org/tyche/orphic-hymn-to-tyche.

Painter, Sally. "Fertility Spells with Candles." Love to Know. (n.d.). https://candles.lovetoknow.com/candle-magic/fertility-spells-candles.

"Reading a Candle." Nurse the Soul. May 30, 2019. https://nursethesoul.com/2019/05/30/reading-a-candle.

Saunders, William. "The History of Votive Candles." Catholic Education Resource Center. 2003. https://www.catholiceducation.org/en/culture/catholic-contributions/the-history-of-votive-candles.html.

Tetrault, Sam. "What Does It Mean to Light a Memorial Candle for the Dead?" Cake. January 7, 2020. https://www.joincake.com/blog/lighting-a-candle-for-someone-who-has-died.

ABOUT THE AUTHORS

Sandra Mariah Wright is a prominent Salem Witch and the High Priestess of Elphame, an Alexandrian coven. She lives with her husband, Kevin; their pug, Abigail; and their two magical kitties, Merlin and Marie Marie, on her family's estate on Gallows Hill in Salem, where 19 people once were hanged for the charge of Witchcraft.

Sandra owns a jewelry and occult supply company, Gallows Hill Witchery, and hosts live crystal and jewelry sales (to the delight of her "Crystal Coven"). She also owns an events business, Spirit Beacon Psychic Fair and Mystical Marketplace, and manages the largest annual psychic fair in the country. She has appeared on the Travel Channel and Showtime and has been featured on *The Real Housewives of New York City*, Chronicle and Dish Network's *Magnificent Obsessions*.

※

Leanne Marrama is a renowned Salem Witch and co-owner of Pentagram with Timothy Reagan at 282 Derby Street in Salem, Massachusetts. She is a High Priestess in the Celtic Traditional Gwyddonaid as well as the Minoan Sisterhood and teaches classes and presents at festivals around the country. Among her many media appearances, she has been featured on TLC's *What Not to Wear*, *Beyond Belief with George Noory*, and the History Channel.

Currently Leanne lives with her partner, Chris, and her Australian cattle dog, Sadie. She is a proud mother of two amazing adult children, Elizabeth and Kevin.

※

On the first Thursday of every month, Sandra and Leanne host *The Psychic Tea*, an hour-long show broadcast live on their Psychic Tea Facebook page, as well as on local radio at 102.9FM HD2. The Astro Forecast on the show is provided by resident astrologer Tim Soaring Wolf. You can find an archive of all their previous shows on their Facebook page.